S0-BOA-791

Level 1

¡Avancemos!

Unit 5 Resource Book

HOLT McDOUGAL
a division of Houghton Mifflin Harcourt

Printed in United States of America

Fine Art Acknowledgments

Page 86 *Canoas y casas en el suburbio (Canoes and Houses in the Suburbs)* (1989), Oswaldo Guayasamín. Oil on canvas, 150 cm x 100 cm. Guayaquil de mis amores Collection, Brussels, Belgium. Courtesy of Fundación Guayasamín, Quito, Ecuador.

Page 87 *Indian Dancers and Musicians* (*Quechua Village, Andes*), Hugo Licta. Photograph by Mireille Vautier/The Art Archive.

Page 88 *Las floristas* (1916), Camilo Egas. Oil on canvas, 97 cm x 155 cm. Courtesy of Museo Nacional del Banco Central del Ecuador, Quito.

Page 89 *The Rodriguez's* (2003), Patssi Valdez. Acrylic on canvas, 36″ x 32″. Courtesy of Patricia Correia Gallery, Santa Monica, CA.

ISBN-13: 978-0-618-76616-1
ISBN-10: 0-618-76616-2 11 12 1689 16 15
4500531933
Internet: www.holtmcdougal.com

HOLT McDOUGAL

¡Avancemos!

Table of Contents

To the Teacher . . . . . vi–xii
Tips for Students . . . . . xiii–xv

DID YOU GET IT? RETEACHING AND PRACTICE COPYMASTERS
Lección 1 1–12
Lección 2 13–24
Answer Key 25–30

PRACTICE GAMES
Lección 1 31–38
Lección 2 39–46
Answer Key 47–50

VIDEO ACTIVITIES COPYMASTERS
Lección 1 51–58
Lección 2 59–66
Answer Key 67–68

VIDEO SCRIPTS
Lección 1 69–70
Lección 2 71–72

AUDIO SCRIPTS
Lección 1 73–77
Lección 2 78–82

MAP/CULTURE ACTIVITIES 83–84
Answer Key 85

FINE ART ACTIVITIES
Lección 1 86–87
Lección 2 88–89
Answer Key 90

FAMILY LETTER 91

FAMILY INVOLVEMENT ACTIVITY 92

ABSENT STUDENT COPYMASTERS
Lección 1 93–100
Lección 2 101–111

To the Teacher

Welcome to *¡Avancemos!* This exciting new Spanish program from McDougal Littell has been designed to provide you—the teacher of today's foreign language classroom—with comprehensive pedagogical support.

PRACTICE WITH A PURPOSE

Activities throughout the program begin by establishing clear goals. Look for the **¡Avanza!** arrow that uses student-friendly language to lead the way towards achievable goals. Built-in self-checks in the student text (**Para y piensa:** Did you get it?) offer the chance to assess student progress throughout the lesson. Both the student text and the workbooks offer abundant leveled practice to match varied student needs.

CULTURE AS A CORNERSTONE

¡Avancemos! celebrates the cultural diversity of the Spanish-speaking world by motivating students to think about similarities and contrasts among different Spanish-speaking cultures. Essential questions encourage thoughtful discussion and comparison between different cultures.

LANGUAGE LEARNING THAT LASTS

The program presents topics in manageable chunks that students will be able to retain and recall. "Recycle" topics are presented frequently so students don't forget material from previous lessons. Previously learned content is built upon and reinforced across the different levels of the program.

TIME-SAVING TEACHER TOOLS

Simplify your planning with McDougal Littell's exclusive teacher resources: the all-inclusive EasyPlanner DVD-ROM, ready-made Power Presentations, and the McDougal Littell Assessment System.

Unit Resource Book

Each Unit Resource Book supports a unit of *¡Avancemos!* The Unit Resource Books provide a wide variety of materials to support, practice, and expand on the material in the *¡Avancemos!* student text.

Components **Following is a list of components included in each Unit Resource Book:**

BACK TO SCHOOL RESOURCES (UNIT 1 ONLY)

Review and start-up activities to support the **Lección preliminar** of the textbook.

DID YOU GET IT? RETEACHING & PRACTICE COPYMASTERS

If students' performance on the **Para y piensa** self-check for a section does not meet your expectations, consider assigning the corresponding Did You Get It? Reteaching and Practice Copymasters. These copymasters provide extensive reteaching and additional practice for every vocabulary and grammar presentation section in *¡Avancemos!* Each vocabulary and grammar section has a corresponding three-page copymaster. The first page of the copymaster reteaches the subject material in a fresh manner. Immediately following this presentation page are two pages of practice exercises that help the student master the topic. The practice pages have engaging contexts and structures to retain students' attention.

PRACTICE GAMES

These games provide fun practice of the vocabulary and grammar just taught. They are targeted in scope so that each game practices a specific area of the **lesson**: *Práctica de vocabulario*, *Vocabulario en contexto*, *Práctica de gramática*, *Gramática en contexto*, *Todo junto*, *Repaso de la lección*, and the lesson's cultural information.

Video and audio resources

VIDEO ACTIVITIES

These two-page copymasters accompany the Vocabulary Video and each scene of the **Telehistoria** in Levels 1 and 2 and the **Gran desafío** in Level 3. The pre-viewing activity asks students to activate prior knowledge about a theme or subject related to the scene they will watch. The viewing activity is a simple activity for students to complete as they watch the video. The post-viewing activity gives students the opportunity to demonstrate comprehension of the video episode.

VIDEO SCRIPTS

This section provides the scripts of each video feature in the unit.

AUDIO SCRIPTS

This section contains scripts for all presentations and activities that have accompanying audio in the student text as well as in the two workbooks (*Cuaderno: práctica por niveles* and *Cuaderno para hispanohablantes*) and the assessment program.

Culture resources

MAP/CULTURE ACTIVITIES

This section contains a copymaster with geography and culture activities based on the Unit Opener in the textbook.

FINE ART ACTIVITIES

The fine art activities in every lesson ask students to analyze pieces of art that have been selected as representative of the unit location country. These copymasters can be used in conjunction with the full-color fine art transparencies in the Unit Transparency Book.

Home-school connection

FAMILY LETTERS & FAMILY INVOLVEMENT ACTIVITIES

This section is designed to help increase family support of the students' study of Spanish. The family letter keeps families abreast of the class's progress, while the family involvement activities let students share their Spanish language skills with their families in the context of a game or fun activity.

ABSENT STUDENT COPYMASTERS

The Absent Student Copymasters enable students who miss part of a **lesson** to go over the material on their own. The checkbox format allows teachers to choose and indicate exactly what material the student should complete. The Absent Student Copymasters also offer strategies and techniques to help students understand new or challenging information.

Core Ancillaries in the ¡Avancemos! Program

Leveled workbooks

CUADERNO: PRÁCTICA POR NIVELES

This core ancillary is a leveled practice workbook to supplement the student text. It is designed for use in the classroom or as homework. Students who can complete the activities correctly should be able to pass the quizzes and tests. Practice is organized into three levels of difficulty, labeled A, B, and C. Level B activities are designed to practice vocabulary, grammar, and other core concepts at a level appropriate to most of your students. Students who require more structure can complete Level A activities, while students needing more of a challenge should be encouraged to complete the activities in Level C. Each level provides a different degree of linguistic support, yet requires students to know and handle the same vocabulary and grammar content.

The following sections are included in *Cuaderno: práctica por niveles* for each **lesson**:

Vocabulario A, B, C
Gramática 1 A, B, C
Gramática 2 A, B, C
Integración: Hablar
Integración: Escribir
Escuchar A, B, C
Leer A, B, C
Escribir A, B, C
Cultura A, B, C

CUADERNO PARA HISPANOHABLANTES

This core ancillary provides leveled practice for heritage learners of Spanish. Level A is for heritage learners who hear Spanish at home but who may speak little Spanish themselves. Level B is for those who speak some Spanish but don't read or write it yet and who may lack formal education in Spanish. Level C is for heritage learners who have had some formal schooling in Spanish. These learners can read and speak Spanish, but may need further development of their writing skills. The *Cuaderno para hispanohablantes* will ensure that heritage learners practice the same basic grammar, reading, and writing skills taught in the student text. At the same time, it offers additional instruction and challenging practice designed specifically for students with prior knowledge of Spanish.

The following sections are included in *Cuaderno para hispanohablantes* for each **lesson**:

Vocabulario A, B, C
Vocabulario adicional
Gramática 1 A, B, C
Gramática 2 A, B, C
Gramática adicional
Integración: Hablar
Integración: Escribir
Lectura A, B, C
Escritura A, B, C
Cultura A, B, C

Other Ancillaries

ASSESSMENT PROGRAM

For each level of *¡Avancemos!*, there are four complete assessment options. Every option assesses students' ability to use the lesson and unit vocabulary and grammar, as well as assessing reading, writing, listening, speaking, and cultural knowledge. The on-level tests are designed to assess the language skills of most of your students. Modified tests provide more support, explanation and scaffolding to enable students with learning difficulties to produce language at the same level as their peers. Pre-AP* tests build the test-taking skills essential to success on Advanced Placement tests. The assessments for heritage learners are all in Spanish, and take into account the strengths that native speakers bring to language learning.

In addition to leveled lesson and unit tests, there is a complete array of vocabulary, culture, and grammar quizzes. All tests include scoring rubrics and point teachers to specific resources for remediation.

UNIT TRANSPARENCY BOOKS—1 PER UNIT

Each transparency book includes:

- Map Atlas Transparencies (Unit 1 only)
- Unit Opener Map Transparencies
- Fine Art Transparencies
- Vocabulary Transparencies
- Grammar Presentation Transparencies
- Situational Transparencies with Label Overlay (plus student copymasters)
- Warm Up Transparencies
- Student Book and Workbook Answer Transparencies

LECTURAS PARA TODOS

A workbook-style reader, *Lecturas para todos*, offers all the readings from the student text as well as additional literary readings in an interactive format. In addition to the readings, they contain reading strategies, comprehension questions, and tools for developing vocabulary.

There are four sections in each *Lecturas para todos*:

- *¡Avancemos!* readings with annotated skill-building support
- *Literatura adicional*—additional literary readings
- Academic and Informational Reading Development
- Test Preparation Strategies

* AP and the Advanced Placement Program are registered trademarks of the College Entrance Examination Board, which was not involved in the production of and does not endorse this product.

LECTURAS PARA HISPANOHABLANTES

Lecturas para hispanohablantes offers additional cultural readings for heritage learners and a rich selection of literary readings. All readings are supported by reading strategies, comprehension questions, tools for developing vocabulary, plus tools for literary analysis.

There are four sections in each *Lecturas para hispanohablantes*:

- *En voces* cultural readings with annotated skill-building support
- *Literatura adicional*—high-interest readings by prominent authors from around the Spanish-speaking world. Selections were chosen carefully to reflect the diversity of experiences Spanish-speakers bring to the classroom.
- Bilingual Academic and Informational Reading Development
- Bilingual Test Preparation Strategies, for success on standardized tests in English

COMIC BOOKS

These fun, motivating comic books are written in a contemporary, youthful style with full-color illustrations. Each comic uses the target language students are learning. There is one 32-page comic book for each level of the program.

TPRS: TEACHING PROFICIENCY THROUGH READING AND STORYTELLING

This book includes an up-to-date guide to TPRS and TPRS stories written by Piedad Gutiérrez that use *¡Avancemos!* lesson-specific vocabulary.

MIDDLE SCHOOL RESOURCE BOOK

- Practice activities to support the 1b Bridge lesson
- Diagnostic and Bridge Unit Tests
- Transparencies
  - Vocabulary Transparencies
  - Grammar Transparencies
  - Answer Transparencies for the Student Text
  - Bridge Warm Up Transparencies
- Audio CDs

LESSON PLANS

- Lesson Plans with suggestions for modifying instruction
- Core and Expansion options clearly noted
- IEP suggested modifications
- Substitute teacher lesson plans

BEST PRACTICES TOOLKIT

Strategies for Effective Teaching

- Research-based Learning Strategies
- Language Learning that Lasts: Teaching for Long-term Retention
- Culture as a Cornerstone/Cultural Comparisons
- English Grammar Connection
- Building Vocabulary
- Developing Reading Skills
- Differentiation
- Best Practices in Teaching Heritage Learners
- Assessment (including Portfolio Assessment, Reteaching and Remediation)
- Best Practices Swap Shop: Favorite Activities for Teaching Reading, Writing, Listening, Speaking
- Reading, Writing, Listening, and Speaking Strategies in the World Languages classroom
- ACTFL Professional Development Articles
- Thematic Teaching
- Best Practices in Middle School

Using Technology in the World Languages Classroom

Tools for Motivation

- Games in the World Languages Classroom
- Teaching Proficiency through Reading and Storytelling
- Using Comic Books for Motivation

Pre-AP and International Baccalaureate

- International Baccalaureate
- Pre-AP

Graphic Organizer Transparencies

- Teaching for Long-term Retention
- Teaching Culture
- Building Vocabulary
- Developing Reading Skills

Absent Student Copymasters—Tips for Students

LISTENING TO CDS AT HOME

- Open your text, workbook, or class notes to the corresponding pages that relate to the audio you will listen to. Read the assignment directions if there are any. Do these steps before listening to the audio selections.
- Listen to the CD in a quiet place. Play the CD loudly enough so that you can hear everything clearly. Keep focused. Play a section several times until you understand it. Listen carefully. Repeat aloud with the CD. Try to sound like the people on the CD. Stop the CD when you need to do so.
- If you are lost, stop the CD. Replay it and look at your notes. Take a break if you are not focusing. Return and continue after a break. Work in short periods of time: 5 or 10 minutes at a time so that you remain focused and energized.

QUESTION/ANSWER SELECTIONS

- If there is a question/answer selection, read the question aloud several times. Write down the question. Highlight the key words, verb endings, and any new words. Look up new words and write their meaning. Then say everything aloud.
- One useful strategy for figuring out questions is to put parentheses around groups of words that go together. For example: **(¿Cuántos niños)(van)(al estadio)(a las tres?)** Read each group of words one at a time. Check for meaning. Write out answers. Highlight key words and verb endings. Say the question aloud. Read the answer aloud. Ask yourself if you wrote what you meant.
- Be sure to say everything aloud several times before moving on to the next question. Check for spelling, verb endings, and accent marks.

FLASHCARDS FOR VOCABULARY

- If you have Internet access, go to ClassZone at classzone.com. All the vocabulary taught in *¡Avancemos!* is available on electronic flashcards. Look for the flashcards in the *¡Avancemos!* section of ClassZone.
- If you don't have Internet access, write the Spanish word or phrase on one side of a 3″× 5″ card, and the English translation on the other side. Illustrate your flashcards when possible. Be sure to highlight any verb endings, accent marks, or other special spellings that will need a bit of extra attention.

GRAMMAR ACTIVITIES

- Underline or highlight all verb endings and adjective agreements. For example: **Nosotros comemos pollo rico.**
- Underline or highlight infinitive endings: **trabajar**.
- Underline or highlight accented letters. Say aloud and be louder on the accented letters. Listen carefully for the loudness. This will remind you where to write your accent mark. For example: **lápiz**, **lápices**, **árbol**, **árboles**
- When writing a sentence, be sure to ask yourself, "What do I mean? What am I trying to say?" Then check your sentence to be sure that you wrote what you wanted to say.
- Mark patterns with a highlighter. For example, for stem-changing verbs, you can draw a "boot" around the letters that change:

v**ue**lvo	volvemos
v**ue**lves	volvéis
v**ue**lve	v**ue**lven

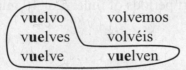

READING AND CULTURE SECTIONS

- Read the strategy box. Copy the graphic organizer so you can fill it out as you read.
- Look at the title and subtitles before you begin to read. Then look at and study any photos and read the captions. Translate the captions only if you can't understand them at all. Before you begin to read, guess what the selection will be about. What do you think that you will learn? What do you already know about this topic?
- Read any comprehension questions before beginning to read the paragraphs. This will help you focus on the upcoming reading selection. Copy the questions and highlight key words.
- Reread one or two of the questions and then go to the text. Begin to read the selection carefully. Read it again. On a sticky note, write down the appropriate question number next to where the answer lies in the text. This will help you keep track of what the questions have asked you and will help you focus when you go back to reread it later, perhaps in preparation for a quiz or test.
- Highlight any new words. Make a list or flashcards of new words. Look up their meanings. Study them. Quiz yourself or have a partner quiz you. Then go back to the comprehension questions and check your answers from memory. Look back at the text if you need to verify your answers.

PAIRED PRACTICE EXERCISES

- If there is an exercise for partners, practice both parts at home.
- If no partner is available, write out both scripts and practice both roles aloud. Highlight and underline key words, verb endings, and accent marks.

WRITING PROJECTS

- Brainstorm ideas before writing.
- Make lists of your ideas.
- Put numbers next to the ideas to determine the order in which you want to write about them.
- Group your ideas into paragraphs.
- Skip lines in your rough draft.
- Have a partner read your work and give you feedback on the meaning and language structure.
- Set it aside and reread it at least once before doing a final draft. Double-check verb endings, adjective agreements, and accents.
- Read it once again to check that you said what you meant to say.
- Be sure to have a title and any necessary illustrations or bibliography.

Did You Get It? *Presentación de vocabulario*

Level 1 **pp. 248–249**
Level 1B **pp. 42–44**

¡AVANZA! **Goal:** Learn to talk about houses.

The House

- All **casas** *(houses)* are different, but they have the same rooms and furniture—and playthings! Read the list of words below that you can use to describe what your house is like.

Rooms
el comedor *(dining room)*
el cuarto *(room, bedroom)*
el suelo *(floor)*
la cocina *(kitchen)*
la sala *(living room)*

Furniture
el espejo *(mirror)*
el sillón *(armchair)*
el sofá *(sofa)*
la alfombra *(rug)*
la cama *(bed)*
la cómoda *(dresser)*
la lámpara *(lamp)*
las cortinas *(curtains)*

Entertainment
el radio *(radio)*
el televisor *(television set)*
el tocadiscos compactos *(CD player)*
los discos compactos *(CDs)*
los videojuegos *(video games)*

Outside the house
el jardín *(garden)*
el patio *(patio)*

- Not everyone lives in a house. Read the paragraph to learn where other people live.

Not everyone in Ecuador or in other countries lives in a large house. For many people, living in **un apartamento** *(apartment)* is **ideal** *(ideal)*. Some people live on **la planta baja** *(ground floor)*. Others live on **el primer piso** *(first floor)*. Still others live on higher floors and have to **subir la escalera** *(climb the stairs)* to reach their floor.

Nombre ______________________ Clase ______________ Fecha ______________

Did You Get It? *Práctica de vocabulario*

***Level 1* p. 250**
***Level 1B* p. 45**

¡AVANZA! **Goal:** Learn to talk about houses.

1 Match the following.

a.

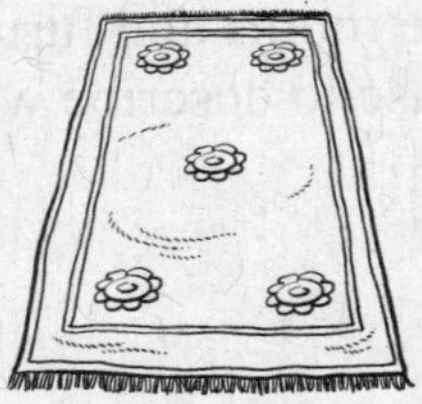
b.

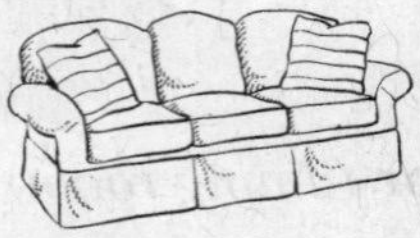
c.

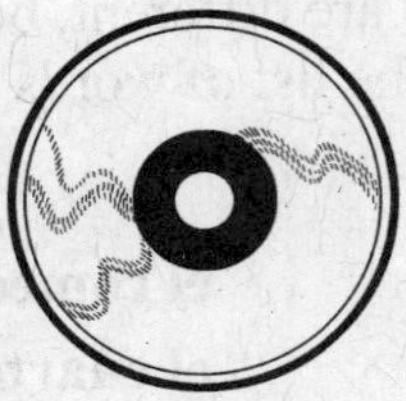
d.

e.

f.

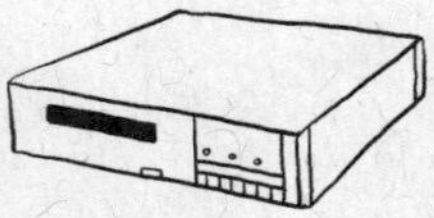
g.

h.

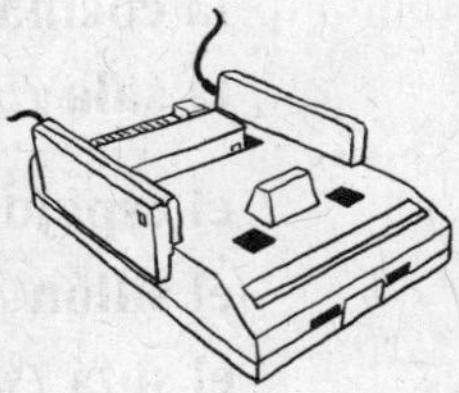
i.

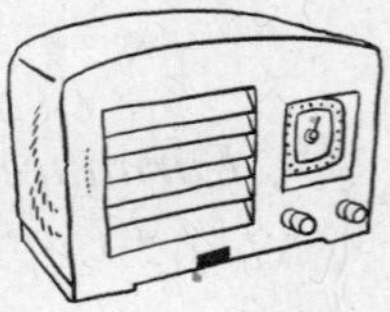
j.

1. _____ el videojuego
2. _____ el radio
3. _____ el espejo
4. _____ la lámpara
5. _____ el tocadiscos compactos
6. _____ la alfombra
7. _____ el sofá
8. _____ las cortinas
9. _____ disco compacto
10. _____ el televisor

2 What do you normally use to…

1. escuchar música?
   las cortinas   la cama   el radio
2. descansar?
   el espejo   las cortinas   el sofá
3. leer?
   la cocina   la alfombra   la lámpara
4. ver programas de televisión?
   la cama   el televisor   el suelo

3 Where do you normally go to…

1. dormir?
   el cuarto   la cocina   el suelo
2. comer?
   el radio   el espejo   el comedor
3. cocinar?
   la cocina   el jardín   el cuarto
4. leer el periódico?
   la sala   el espejo   el radio

4 Choose a word from the box to explain where these people are. You can use each place more than one time.

la sala	**el comedor**	**la cocina**	**el jardín**	**el patio**	**el cuarto**

1. Juan come. ______
2. Antonio descansa. ______
3. Julio prepara una barbacoa. ______
4. Eva planta flores *(flowers)*. ______
5. El señor Tobar lee el periódico. ______
6. Ana escucha un disco compacto. ______
7. Beatriz toca el piano. ______
8. Nosotros miramos la televisión. ______
9. Yo como cereal. ______
10. El chico habla por teléfono. ______

5 Choose a word from the box to complete each sentence.

cuarto	**alfombras**	**comedor**	**tocadiscos compactos**	**lámpara**	**cocina**

1. Uso una ______ para leer.
2. Preparo la comida en la ______.
3. Siempre estudio en mi ______.
4. Voy al ______ para comer.
5. Para escuchar música, uso el ______.
6. Tenemos unas ______ bonitas en el suelo.

6 Write a short paragraph describing your house and some of the things in it.

Modelo: *Mi casa es grande. Tiene tres pisos. También tiene un jardín muy bonito. En la sala hay un televisor. En mi cuarto hay otro televisor. También hay un tocadiscos compactos. Miro la televisión y escucho música en mi cuarto.*

______

______

______

______

Nombre ______________________ Clase ______________ Fecha ______________

Did You Get It? *Presentación de gramática*

***Level 1* p. 253**
***Level 1B* p. 48**

¡AVANZA! **Goal:** Learn the differences between **ser** and **estar**.

Ser and *estar*

- There are two verbs in Spanish that mean *to be*. Read the sentences below, paying attention to the boldfaced verb in each. As you read each set of sentences, think about what they are about.

*I **am** from the United States.*	→	*origin*	→	Yo **soy** de Estados Unidos.
*The girls **are** nice.*	→	*trait*	→	Las chicas **son** simpáticas.
*Raúl **is** an actor.*	→	*profession*	→	Raúl **es** actor.
*It **is** one o'clock.*	→	*time*	→	**Es** la una.
*The CDs **are** Alex's.*	→	*possession*	→	Los discos compactos **son** de Alex.
*It **is** January 1st.*	→	*date*	→	**Es** el primero de enero.

- Now read this set of sentences.

*I **am** in Spanish class.*	→	*location*	→	Yo **estoy** en la clase de español.
*The boys **are** fine.*	→	*physical condition*	→	Los chicos **están** bien.
*The girls **are** happy.*	→	*emotional condition*	→	Las chicas **están** contentas.

EXPLANATION: Ser and **estar** both mean *to be*. There are six situations when you use **ser**: (1) to indicate origin, or where someone is from; (2) to describe personal traits or physical characteristics; (3) to indicate professions; (4) to tell time; (5) to indicate possession; and (6) to give the date. There are three situations when you use **estar**: (1) to say where someone or something is; (2) to describe a physical condition (usually health-related states); and (3) to describe an emotional condition (usually feelings).

Nombre ______________________ Clase ______________ Fecha ______________

Did You Get It? *Práctica de gramática*

Level 1 **pp. 254–255**
Level 1B **pp. 49–51**

¡AVANZA! **Goal:** Learn the differences between **ser** and **estar**.

1 Answer the questions using the model as a guide.

Modelo: ¿De dónde es Juan? (de Quito)
Juan es de Quito.

1. ¿Cómo es Luis? (simpático) ______________________
2. ¿De dónde es Andrea? (de Guayaquil) ______________________
3. ¿Cómo es el libro? (interesante) ______________________
4. ¿Cómo son los chicos? (inteligentes) ______________________
5. ¿Cómo es la clase de español? (divertida) ______________________
6. ¿De quién es el disco compacto? (de Jorge) ______________________
7. ¿Qué hora es? (1:30) ______________________
8. ¿Qué fecha es hoy? (4 de enero) ______________________
9. ¿Cómo son los chicos? (altos) ______________________
10. ¿Qué es la señora López? (maestra) ______________________

2 Answer the questions following the model.

Modelo: ¿Dónde está Juan? (en la escuela)
Juan está en la escuela.

1. ¿Cómo está Linda? (bien) ______________________
2. ¿Dónde está Quito? (en Ecuador) ______________________
3. ¿Cómo están Paco y Ana? (cansados) ______________________
4. ¿Dónde está París? (en Francia) ______________________
5. ¿Cómo está Pedro? (triste) ______________________

3 In the following sentences, which verb would you use, **ser** or **estar**?

1. María is tall. ______________
2. Tomás is worried. ______________
3. I am tired. ______________
4. They are in the garden. ______________
5. We are students. ______________
6. Eduardo is studious. ______________
7. My sister is pretty. ______________
8. My mother is in the car. ______________
9. Anita is a brunette. ______________
10. I am from Spain. ______________

Nombre ______________________ Clase ______________ Fecha ______________

❹ Complete each sentence with the correct form of **ser** or **estar**.

1. Nosotros ____________ en la sala.
2. La lámpara ____________ de Quito.
3. Los jardines ____________ bonitos.
4. Va a su cuarto porque ____________ cansado.
5. Ellos ____________ en la cocina.
6. ____________ las seis de la tarde.
7. Mi casa ____________ al lado de su casa.
8. Luis ____________ alto.

❺ Translate the following sentences into Spanish.

1. The fruit is from Florida. ____________
2. My brothers are in the kitchen. ____________
3. María's dog is lazy. ____________
4. Mr. Velázquez is a teacher. ____________
5. María is studious. ____________
6. Today is July 4th. ____________
7. It is three o'clock. ____________

❻ Use complete sentences to answer these questions about you, your house, and your Spanish class.

Sobre ti

1. ¿Cómo eres? ____________
2. ¿De dónde eres? ____________
3. ¿Cómo estás hoy? ____________
4. ¿Dónde estás ahora? ____________

Tu casa

5. ¿Cómo es tu casa? ____________
6. ¿Dónde está tu casa? ____________

Tu clase de español

7. ¿Cómo es tu clase de español? ____________
8. ¿A qué hora es tu clase de español? ____________

Did You Get It? *Presentación de gramática*

Level 1 p. 258
Level 1B p. 54

¡AVANZA! **Goal:** Learn ordinal numbers.

Ordinal numbers

- **Ordinal numbers** indicate position *(first, second, third)* in a series or the order of items. Read the sentences below, paying attention to the boldfaced words, and to their placement in the sentences.

  Magda vive en la **primera casa.** *(Magda lives in the **first house**.)*
  Andrés vive en el **sexto piso.** *(Andrés lives on the **sixth floor**.)*

EXPLANATION: As in English, ordinal numbers in Spanish are placed *before* nouns. Ordinal numbers agree in gender and number with the nouns they describe. In the first sentence, **primera** agrees with the feminine noun **casa**. In the second sentence, **sexto** agrees with the masculine noun **piso**.

- Now read these sentences, paying attention to the boldfaced words.

  Enero es el **primer** mes del año. *(January is the **first** month of the year.)*
  Marzo es el **tercer** mes del año. *(March is the **third** month of the year.)*

EXPLANATION: **Primero** and **tercero** drop the **o** before a masculine singular noun, such as **mes**. Study the chart below and use it as a quick reference for ordinal numbers.

Ordinal Numbers	
primero(a) *(first)* **primer** *(before a masc. sing. noun)* **segundo(a)** *(second)* **tercero(a)** *(third)* **tercer** *(before a masc. sing. noun)* **cuarto(a)** *(fourth)* **quinto(a)** *(fifth)*	**sexto(a)** *(sixth)* **séptimo(a)** *(seventh)* **octavo(a)** *(eighth)* **noveno(a)** *(ninth)* **décimo(a)** *(tenth)*

Nombre ______________________ Clase ____________ Fecha ____________

UNIDAD 5 Lección 1

Reteaching and Practice

Did You Get It? *Práctica de gramática*

Level 1 **pp. 259–260**
Level 1B **pp. 55–57**

¡AVANZA! **Goal:** Learn ordinal numbers.

1 On which floor does each person live? Complete the sentences using the model as a guide.

Modelo: Antonio vive en el *cuarto* piso. *(4)*

1. Lupe vive en el ____________ piso. *(1)*
2. Marisa vive en el ____________ piso. *(9)*
3. Óscar y María viven en el ____________ piso. *(6)*
4. La familia Suárez vive en el ____________ piso. *(3)*
5. Mi amigo vive en el ____________ piso. *(5)*
6. La maestra de español vive en el ____________ piso. *(7)*
7. Los chicos viven en el ____________ piso. *(2)*
8. Mis abuelos viven en el ____________ piso. *(10)*
9. Pilar vive en el ____________ piso. *(8)*

2 Who is wearing what? Follow the model to answer the questions.

Modelo: ¿Quién lleva un sombrero?
La sexta persona lleva un sombrero.

1. ¿Quién lleva pantalones cortos? ______________________
2. ¿Quién lleva una chaqueta? ______________________
3. ¿Quién lleva una camiseta? ______________________
4. ¿Quién lleva un vestido? ______________________
5. ¿Quién lleva un traje? ______________________
6. ¿Quién lleva jeans? ______________________
7. ¿Quién lleva una blusa? ______________________
8. ¿Quién lleva un gorro? ______________________

Nombre ______________________ Clase ______________________ Fecha ______________________

3 Look at the picture and answer the following questions.

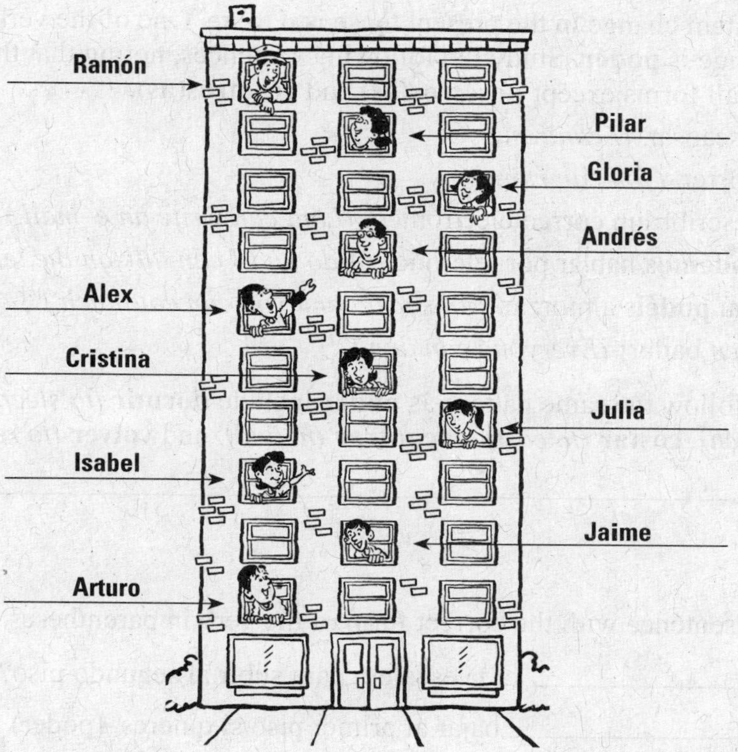

To which floor do you go to visit each person? Follow the model.

Modelo: ¿A Jaime? *Voy al segundo piso.*

1. ¿a Álex? ______________________
2. ¿a Arturo? ______________________
3. ¿a Isabel? ______________________
4. ¿a Ramón? ______________________
5. ¿a Cristina? ______________________
6. ¿a Gloria? ______________________
7. ¿a Pilar? ______________________
8. ¿a Julia? ______________________
9. ¿a Andrés? ______________________

4 Translate the following sentences into Spanish.

1. I live in the fourth house on Elm Street.

____

2. The second book is Margarita's.

____

Nombre ______________________ Clase ______________ Fecha ______________

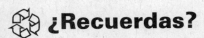

Level 1 p. 250
Level 1B p. 45

¿Recuerdas?

Stem-changing verbs o → ue

- A common verb stem change in the present tense is **o** to **ue**. One of the verbs that has this stem change is **poder**. Study the following sentences, noting that the stem change occurs in all forms except **nosotros(as)** and **vosotros(as)**.

  Yo *puedo* descansar. *(I can rest.)*

  Tú *puedes* correr. *(You can run.)*

  Lola *puede* escribir un correo electrónico. *(Lola can write an e–mail.)*

  Aldo y yo **podemos** hablar por teléfono. *(Aldo and I can talk on the telephone.)*

  Anastasia y tú **podéis** almorzar. *(Anastasia and you can eat lunch.)*

  ¡Todos *pueden* bailar! *(Everyone can dance!)*

- Other verbs that follow the same pattern as **poder** include **dormir** *(to sleep)*, **almorzar** *(to lunch)*, **costar** *(to cost)*, **encontrar** *(to find)*, and **volver** *(to return)*.

Práctica

1 Complete each sentence with the correct form of the verb in parentheses.

1. ¿ ______________________ tú la escalera para subir al segundo piso? (encontrar)
2. Yo ______________________ bajar al primer piso si quieres. (poder)
3. Roberto y yo ______________________ en casa de José. (dormir)
4. Vosotros ______________________ a las doce y media. (almorzar)
5. ¿Cuánto ______________________ la lámpara? (costar)
6. Lupe ______________________ del cine a las nueve y media. (volver)
7. Nosotros ______________________ una cómoda bonita para el cuarto. (encontrar)
8. ¿ ______________________ nosotros subir la escalera para llegar al tercer piso? (poder)
9. Yo ______________________ en el nuevo restaurante. (almorzar)
10. Tú y Linda ______________________ mucho generalmente. (dormir)

2 Write sentences using the verbs and subjects given.

1. (almorzar) Yo ____
2. (poder) Tú ____
3. (volver) Mis amigos ____
4. (dormir) Mis padres ____
5. (encontrar) Mi mejor amigo ____

Nombre ______________________ Clase ______________ Fecha ______________

¿Recuerdas?

Level 1 p. 254
Level 1B p. 49

Location words

- Review the following expressions to talk about location in Spanish.

lejos de *(far from)*	⟷	**cerca de** *(near to)*
delante de *(in front of)*	⟷	**detrás de** *(behind)*
encima de *(on top of)*	⟷	**debajo de** *(under)*
al lado de *(next to)*	⟷	**dentro de** *(inside of)*

Práctica

Use the location words above to describe where the following items are in relation to each other. Follow the model.

Modelo: la lámpara / la mesa
La lámpara está encima de la mesa.

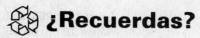

1. la alfombra / el sofá ______________________
2. el sillón / la ventana ______________________
3. las cortinas / la ventana ______________________
4. la computadora / el escritorio ______________________
5. el sillón / el sofá ______________________
6. el escritorio / la sala ______________________
7. el espejo / la ventana ______________________
8. la lámpara / el sillón ______________________
9. el sofá / la televisión ______________________

¿Recuerdas?

Level 1 pp. 255, 259
Level 1B pp. 50, 55

Colors

- Review and study the following names of colors in Spanish.

amarillo(a) *(yellow)*
anaranjado(a) *(orange)*
azul *(pl.,* **azules***)* *(blue)*
blanco(a) *(white)*
marrón *(pl.,* **marrones***)* *(brown)*
negro(a) *(black)*
rojo(a) *(red)*
verde *(green)*

Clothing

- Review the following Spanish words for clothes.

Para los chicos

la camisa *(shirt)*

Para todos

el gorro *(winter hat)*
el sombrero *(hat)*
la camiseta *(T-shirt)*
la chaqueta *(jacket)*
los calcetines *(socks)*
los jeans *(jeans)*
los pantalones *(pants)*
los pantalones cortos *(shorts)*
los zapatos *(shoes)*

Para las chicas

el vestido *(dress)*
la blusa *(blouse)*

Práctica

Complete the translation of the following sentences. The first one is done for you.

1. Andrés lleva *(blue pants)* *pantalones azules*.
2. Los chicos llevan *(black jeans)* ______.
3. Yo llevo *(a yellow dress)* ______.
4. En el verano, llevas *(a white T-shirt)* ______.
5. Tú llevas *(a green blouse)* ______.
6. En el invierno, llevamos *(black hats)* ______.
7. Cuando hace frío, lleváis *(a brown jacket)* ______.
8. Nosotros llevamos *(red shorts)* ______.
9. Cuando hace calor, él lleva *(a white hat)* ______.
10. ¡Jorge siempre lleva *(orange shoes)* ______!

Nombre ______________________ Clase ______________ Fecha ______________

Did You Get It? *Presentación de vocabulario*

Level 1 **pp. 272–273**
Level 1B **pp. 70–72**

¡AVANZA! **Goal:** Learn how to talk about planning a party.

The surprise party

- There are many things to do when you want to to give a party (**dar una fiesta**). If it's a surprise party (**una fiesta de sorpresa**), you first need to ask everyone to keep the secret (**el secreto**). Then you must clean (**hay que limpiar**) the house before the guests (**los invitados**) arrive. It's probably best to make a list of chores (**los quehaceres**) that need to be done to get the house in order. After all, you wouldn't want to invite people to a house that is dirty (**sucia**)! Here are some suggestions to study.

  cortar el césped *(to cut the grass)*
  hacer la cama *(to make the bed)*
  pasar la aspiradora *(to vacuum)*
  planchar la ropa *(to iron)*
  limpiar la cocina *(to clean the kitchen)*
  lavar los platos *(to wash the dishes)*
  barrer el suelo *(to sweep the floor)*
  sacar la basura *(to take out the trash)*

- Once the house is **limpia** (clean) and in order, you should decorate it (**debes decorarla**). Your friends will probably volunteer to help (**ayudar**) because decorating is fun. The decorations (**las decoraciones**) can include streamers and balloons (**globos**). It's important to put up the decorations (**poner las decoraciones**) and set the table (**poner la mesa**) before starting to cook (**cocinar**). And don't forget to feed the dog (**darle de comer al perro**). You certainly don't want him to eat the party food while you're in the living room putting together the gift (**el regalo**) for your friend.

-  After you wrap (**envolver**) your friend's gift with gift paper (**el papel de regalo**), you can relax, but not for too long.

- Your friends like to come (**venir**) early and celebrate (**celebrar**) right away. So, when the guest of honor arrives, be ready to say (**decir**) «¡Sorpresa!» and to begin to dance (**bailar**) and sing (**cantar**), and eat the food that you just prepared (**acabas de preparar**). That is, if you remembered to feed the dog!

Did You Get It? *Práctica de vocabulario*

***Level 1* p. 274**
***Level 1B* p. 73**

¡AVANZA! **Goal:** Learn how to talk about planning a party.

1 What do you do when…

1. there are crumbs on the kitchen floor?
   barrer el suelo   cortar el césped
2. the carpet is dirty?
   hacer la cama   pasar la aspiradora
3. the dishes are piled high in the sink?
   sacar la basura   lavar los platos
4. the grass is overgrown?
   cortar el césped   limpiar la cocina
5. the bed is unmade?
   sacar la basura   hacer la cama
6. the trash is overflowing?
   limpiar la cocina   sacar la basura
7. the clothes are wrinkled?
   cortar el césped   planchar la ropa

2 Write a sentence explaining what one should do based on each picture. Follow the model.

Modelo: *Hay que pasar la aspiradora.*

1.

2.

3.

4.

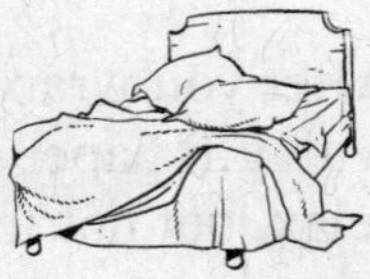
5.

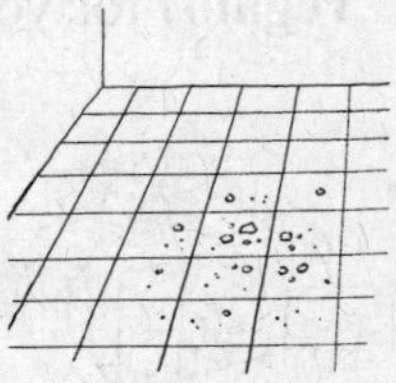
6.

1. ____.
2. ____.
3. ____.
4. ____.
5. ____.
6. ____.

Nombre ______________________ Clase ______________ Fecha ______________

3 Complete the paragraphs with words and expressions from the box.

ayudar	**celebrar**	**cocinar**	**dar una fiesta**	**decir**
envolver	**la aspiradora**	**bailar**	**las decoraciones**	**limpia**
globos	**los invitados**	**los platos**	**sorpresa**	**venir**

Hoy es el cumpleaños de Marisa. Vamos a **1.** ______________, pero es un secreto. Sí, ¡es una fiesta de **2.** ______________!

3. ______________ van a **4.** ______________ a las siete. Tenemos que trabajar mucho.

La casa está sucia y debe estar **5.** ______________. Mi familia va a **6.** ______________.

Mi hermano Juan va a lavar **7.** ______________, barrer el suelo y pasar **8.** ______________. Mi hermana Luisa va a poner **9.** ______________. Ella tiene **10.** ______________ de muchos colores. Mi mamá va a **11.** ______________ una buena comida y mi papá va a hacer el pastel. ¿Y yo? Yo voy a **12.** ______________ los regalos para Marisa.

Cuando llega Marisa, todos vamos a **13.** ______________ «¡Sorpresa!» y «¡Feliz cumpleaños!» Vamos a **14.** ______________ con muchas cosas ricas y muchos platos y dulces deliciosos. También vamos a **15.** ______________ y cantar.

4 Choose a logical response for each statement in the left column.

1. ____ La cocina está sucia.

2. ____ Voy a poner las decoraciones.

3. ____ El perro tiene hambre.

4. ____ Hoy es mi cumpleaños.

5. ____ ¿Quieres envolver el regalo?

6. ____ ¿Te gusta poner la mesa?

a. Voy a darle de comer ahora.

b. Sí, ¿dónde está el papel?

c. Voy a limpiarla.

d. ¡Feliz cumpleaños!

e. Sí, ¿dónde están los platos?

f. Gracias. Aquí tienes los globos.

5 Use **Hay que** + *infinitive* to write, in order, five things one must do to prepare for a party.

1. ____

2. ____

3. ____

4. ____

5. ____

Did You Get It? *Presentación de gramática*

Level 1 p. 277
Level 1B p. 76

¡AVANZA! **Goal:** Learn the forms of more irregular verbs.

More irregular verbs

- Read and study the following sentences, paying attention to the boldfaced words.

Yo **digo** la verdad. *(I **say** the truth.)*
Tú **dices** que es una fiesta sorpresa. *(You **say** that it's a surprise party.)*
Ella **dice** que es un secreto. *(She **says** that it's a secret.)*
Ana y tú **decís** que os gustan los regalos. *(Ana and you **say** that you like the gifts.)*
¡Todos **dicen** que es una buena fiesta! *(Everyone **says** that it is a good party!)*
Nosotros **decimos** que la decoraciones son divertidas. *(We **say** that the decorations are fun.)*

- Study these sentences, paying attention to the boldfaced verbs.

Yo **vengo** a las seis. *(I **come** at six o'clock.)*
Tú **vienes** a las seis y media. *(You **come** at 6:30.)*
¿A qué hora **viene** él? *(What time does he **come**?)*
Nosotros **venimos** a las siete. *(We **come** at seven o'clock.)*
Paco y tú **venís** a las siete y cuarto. *(Paco and you **come** at 7:15.)*
¡Todos **vienen** temprano! *(All **come** early!)*

EXPLANATION: Decir and **venir** have several irregular forms. Only the **nosotros(as)** and **vosotros(as)** forms are regular. Use the chart below as a quick reference for the conjugation of **decir** and **venir** in the present tense.

Infinitive	**decir** *(to say, to tell)*	**venir** *(to come)*
yo	**digo** *(I say)*	**vengo** *(I come)*
tú	**dices** *(you say)*	**vienes** *(you come)*
usted	**dice** *(you say)*	**viene** *(you come)*
él/ella	**dice** *(he/she says)*	**viene** *(he/she comes)*
nosotros(as)	**decimos** *(we say)*	**venimos** *(we come)*
vosotros(as)	**decís** *(you say)*	**venís** *(you come)*
ellos(as)/ustedes	**dicen** *(they/you say)*	**vienen** *(they/you come)*

- Read the following sentences, paying attention to the boldfaced words.

Doy una fiesta de cumpleaños. ***(I am giving** a birthday party.)*
¿**Pongo** la mesa ahora? ***(Do I set** the table now?)*
Salgo para la fiesta a las siete. ***(I am leaving** for the party at seven o'clock.)*
¿**Traigo** los discos compactos a la fiesta? ***(Do I bring** the CDs to the party?)*

EXPLANATION: The verbs **dar, poner, salir,** and **traer** are irregular only in the **yo** form.

Nombre ______________________ Clase ______________ Fecha ______________

Did You Get It? *Práctica de gramática*

Level 1 **pp. 278–279**
Level 1B **pp. 77–79**

¡AVANZA! **Goal:** Learn the forms of more irregular verbs.

1 Write the correct form of **decir** for each subject.

yo ______________________ tú ______________________
los estudiantes ______________________ Pilar ______________________
vosotras ______________________

2 Write the correct form of **venir** for each subject.

vosotros ______________________ la maestra ______________________
ustedes ______________________ yo ______________________
Rodrigo y yo ______________________

3 Write the correct form of **traer** for each subject.

vosotras ______________________ usted ______________________
tú ______________________ yo ______________________
ellos ______________________

4 Write the correct form of **poner** for each subject.

yo ______________________ tú ______________________
usted ______________________ usted ______________________
Anita y yo ______________________

5 Write the correct form of **dar** for each subject.

tú ______________________ usted ______________________
ellos ______________________ Anita y yo ______________________
yo ______________________

6 Write the correct form of **salir** for each subject.

nosotros ______________________ usted ______________________
ellos ______________________ tú ______________________
yo ______________________

7 Write sentences describing who does what for the party. Follow the model.

Modelo: Ariana / venir / a las seis para ayudar
Ariana viene a las seis para ayudar.

1. tú / salir / temprano de casa
____
2. mi hermana / poner / la mesa
____
3. yo / poner / los globos en la sala
____
4. los invitados / venir / a las siete
____
5. todos / decir / «¡Feliz cumpleaños!»
____
6. nosotros / dar / muchos regalos
____

8 Complete the conversation with the correct form of the appropriate verb.

venir	salir	traer	dar	decir	poner

Ana: Félix, tú sabes que hoy _______________ una fiesta para Elena. ¿Cuándo _______________ con las decoraciones?

Félix: _______________ de mi casa en diez minutos. Llego en media hora.

Ana: ¿ _______________ los globos?

Félix: Sí, los llevo. ¿Y tú, Ana, ¿qué haces?

Ana: Yo preparo la comida y _______________ la mesa.

Félix: Y cuando _______________ Elena, todos nosotros _______________ «¡Sorpresa!» y le _______________ los regalos.

9 Write sentences describing four things you do to prepare for a party. Follow the model.

Modelo: salir para comprar un regalo *Salgo para comprar un regalo.*

1. traer los discos compactos _______________.
2. poner las decoraciones _______________.
3. decir «¡Sorpresa!» _______________.
4. dar un regalo _______________.

Nombre ______________________ Clase ______________ Fecha ______________

Did You Get It? *Presentación de gramática*

Level 1 p. 282
Level 1B p. 82

¡AVANZA! **Goal:** Learn how to use affirmative **tú** commands.

Affirmative tú commands

- Giving a command is telling someone what to do. Study the following commands, paying attention to the boldfaced words.

¡**Estudia** la lección! *(**Study** the lesson!)*
¡**Aprende** español! *(**Learn** Spanish!)*
¡**Escribe** la carta! *(**Write** the letter!)*

EXPLANATION: Regular affirmative **tú** commands use the **él/ella/usted** form in the present tense. Study the following chart of affirmative **tú** commands.

Infinitive	Present Tense	Affirmative *tú* Command
estudiar *(to study)* **hablar** *(to speak)*	(Él/ella) **estudia**. *(He/she studies.)* (Él/ella) **habla**. *(He/she speaks.)*	¡**Estudia!** *(Study!)* ¡**Habla!** *(Speak!)*
aprender *(to learn)* **correr** *(to run)*	(Él/ella) **aprende**. *(He/she learns.)* (Él/ella) **corre**. *(He/she runs.)*	¡**Aprende!** *(Learn!)* ¡**Corre!** *(Run!)*
escribir *(to write)* **subir** *(to climb)*	(Él/ella) **escribe**. *(He/she writes.)* (Él/ella) **sube**. *(He/she climbs.)*	¡**Escribe!** *(Write!)* ¡**Sube!** *(Climb!)*

- Read these commands, paying attention to the boldfaced words.

¡Estudia **la lección**! *(Study **the lesson**.)* → ¡Estúdia**la**! *(Study **it**.)*

¡Aprende **los verbos**! *(Learn **the verbs**.)* → ¡Apréndé**los**! *(Learn **them**.)*

¡Escribe **la carta**! *(Write **the letter**.)* → ¡Escríbe**la**! *(Write **it**.)*

EXPLANATION: When using a command with a *direct object pronoun*, *attach* the pronoun to the end. To retain the original stress, add an *accent* when you attach a pronoun to a command of two or more syllables.

Nombre ______________ Clase ______________ Fecha ______________

Did You Get It? *Práctica de gramática*

***Level 1* pp. 283–284**
***Level 1B* pp. 83–85**

¡AVANZA! **Goal:** Learn how to use affirmative **tú** commands.

1 Write the affirmative **tú** command for each of the following **-ar** verbs.

1. bailar ______________
2. cantar ______________
3. cerrar ______________
4. decorar ______________
5. jugar ______________
6. llegar ______________
7. llevar ______________
8. almorzar ______________
9. escuchar ______________
10. celebrar ______________

2 Write the affirmative **tú** command for each of the following **-er** verbs.

1. aprender ______________
2. barrer ______________
3. beber ______________
4. comer ______________
5. correr ______________
6. querer ______________
7. traer ______________
8. vender ______________
9. volver ______________

3 Write the affirmative **tú** command for each of the following **-ir** verbs.

1. compartir ______________
2. dormir ______________
3. escribir ______________
4. recibir ______________
5. abrir ______________
6. vivir ______________

Nombre ______________ Clase ______________ Fecha ______________

❹ Write the affirmative **tú** command for each of the following irregular verbs.

1. poner ______________
2. hacer ______________
3. ser ______________
4. tener ______________
5. ir ______________
6. salir ______________
7. venir ______________
8. decir ______________

❺ Change each infinitive phrase to an affirmative **tú** command. Follow the model.

Modelo: lavar los platos *Lava los platos, por favor.*

1. sacar tus apuntes ______________.
2. envolver el regalo ______________.
3. servir el pastel ______________.
4. cerrar la puerta ______________.
5. poner las decoraciones ______________.
6. llegar temprano ______________.
7. aprender español ______________.
8. beber el jugo ______________.
9. vender la casa ______________.
10. compartir el helado ______________.

❻ Answer each question using an affirmative **tú** command. Follow the model.

Modelo: ¿Debo lavar los platos? *Sí, lávalos, por favor.*

1. ¿Debo servir el postre? ______________.
2. ¿Debo pedir la cuenta? ______________.
3. ¿Debo hacer el pastel? ______________.
4. ¿Debo barrer el suelo? ______________.
5. ¿Debo poner la mesa? ______________.
6. ¿Debo comprar los globos? ______________.
7. ¿Debo vender los libros? ______________.
8. ¿Debo pasar la aspiradora? ______________.
9. ¿Debo cortar el césped? ______________.
10. ¿Debo traer los DVDs? ______________.

¿Recuerdas?

Level 1 pp. 276, 279
Level 1B pp. 75, 79

Tener que and interrogative words

- Read the following questions and answers with **tener que** (*to have to do something*), paying attention to the boldfaced words.

—¿**Qué tiene que hacer** Linda? —**Tiene que comprar** un pastel.	***(What does** Linda **have to do?)*** ***(She has to buy** a cake.)*
—¿**Cuándo** lo **tiene que comprar**? —Lo **tiene que comprar** esta tarde.	***(When does she have to buy** it?)* ***(She has to buy** it this afternoon.)*
—¿**Dónde** lo **tiene que comprar**? —Lo **tiene que comprar** en la pastelería.	***(Where does she have to buy** it?)* ***(She has to buy** it at the bakery.)*
—¿**Por qué** lo **tiene que comprar**? —Lo **tiene que comprar** porque es el cumpleaños de su hermana.	***(Why does she have to buy** it?)* ***(She has to buy** it because it's her sister's birthday.)*
—¿**Cuánto tiene que pagar**? —**Tiene que pagar** ocho dólares.	***(How much does she have to pay?)*** ***(She has to pay** eight dollars.)*
—¿**Cómo lo tienen que envolver**? —Lo **tienen que envolver** con papel de regalo.	***(How do they have to wrap** it?)* ***(They have to wrap it** with gift paper.)*

Práctica

Complete each dialogue with the correct question word.

1. —¿ ____________________ tiene que ir Paula?
—Tiene que ir al centro.

2. —¿ ____________________ tenemos que limpiar la cocina?
—Tienen que limpiar la cocina porque está sucia.

3. —¿ ____________________ tienes que dar la fiesta para Luz?
—Tengo que dar la fiesta el día de su cumpleaños.

4. —¿ ____________________ tiempo tienen que estar ellos en la escuela?
—Tienen que estar allí por tres horas.

5. —¿ ____________________ tengo que ir a la fiesta?
—Tienes que ir en autobús.

6. —¿ ____________________ tiene que comprar Luis?
—Tiene que comprar un regalo de cumpleaños.

Nombre ______________________ Clase ______________ Fecha ______________

¿Recuerdas?

Level 1 p. 281
Level 1B p. 81

Expressions of frequency

- Review the expressions of frequency listed below.

siempre → **todos los días** → **muchas veces** → **mucho** → **de vez en cuando** → **nunca**
(always) *(every day)* *(often, many times)* *(a lot)* *(once in a while)* *(never)*

Práctica

1 Write how often you do each of the following activities.

1. cantar ______________________
2. bailar ______________________
3. dar una fiesta ______________________
4. poner la mesa ______________________
5. salir con amigos ______________________
6. hacer pasteles ______________________
7. limpiar la cocina ______________________
8. hacer tu cama ______________________
9. comprar regalos ______________________
10. estudiar todo el día ______________________

2 Write six sentences naming six things you do, from the most frequent to the least frequent. Use each expression of frequency listed above only once. Follow the model.

Modelo: *Yo siempre hago mi cama antes de salir de casa.*

1. ______________________
2. ______________________
3. ______________________
4. ______________________
5. ______________________
6. ______________________

¿Recuerdas?

Level 1 p. 283
Level 1B p. 83

Direct object pronouns

- Study the following sentences, paying attention to the boldfaced words. Then, review the chart below that contains the direct object pronouns in Spanish.

Voy a limpiar **la cocina**. → Voy a limpiar**la**. or **La** voy a limpiar.

*(I am going to clean **the kitchen**.)* → *(I am going to clean **it**.)*

Direct object pronouns	
Singular	**Plural**
me *(me)*	**nos** *(us)*
te *(you) (familiar)*	**os** *(you) (familiar)*
lo *(you/him/it) (formal)*	**los** *(you formal/them masculine)*
la *(you/her/it) (formal)*	**las** *(you formal/them feminine)*

Práctica

1 Write the direct object pronoun that corresponds with each noun. The first one is done for you.

1. yo *me*
2. las decoraciones ______________
3. el regalo ______________
4. la maestra ______________
5. tú y Alex *(España)* ______________
6. los señores Tobar ______________
7. tú, Rogelio ______________
8. Roque y yo ______________

2 Answer each question with an affirmative **tú** command. Follow the model.

Modelo: ¿Compro el regalo? *Sí, cómpralo, por favor.*

1. ¿Hago el pastel? ______________.
2. ¿Limpio la cocina? ______________.
3. ¿Pongo las decoraciones? ______________.
4. ¿Paso la aspiradora? ______________.
5. ¿Lavo los platos? ______________.
6. ¿Saco la basura? ______________.
7. ¿Preparo las decoraciones? ______________.
8. ¿Envuelvo el regalo? ______________.
9. ¿Corto el césped? ______________.
10. ¿Traigo los DVDs? ______________.

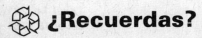

Did You Get It? Answer Key

PRÁCTICA DE VOCABULARIO,
Houses, pp. 2–3

1

1. i
2. j
3. a
4. e
5. g
6. b
7. c
8. f
9. d
10. h

2

1. el radio
2. el sofá
3. la lámpara
4. el televisor

3

1. el cuarto
2. el comedor
3. la cocina
4. la sala

4

1. la cocina / el comedor
2. el cuarto
3. el patio
4. el jardín
5. la sala
6. el cuarto / la sala
7. la sala
8. la sala / el cuarto
9. la cocina / el comedor
10. el cuarto / el jardín / el cuarto / la sala...

5

1. lámpara
2. cocina
3. cuarto
4. comedor
5. tocadiscos compactos
6. alfombras

6 Answers will vary.

PRÁCTICA DE GRAMÁTICA
***Ser** and **estar**, pp. 5–6*

1

1. Luis es simpático.
2. Andrea es de Guayaquil.
3. El libro es interesante.
4. Los chicos son inteligentes.
5. La clase de español es divertida.
6. El disco compacto es de Jorge.
7. Es la una y media.
8. Es el 4 de enero.
9. Los chicos son altos.
10. La señora López es maestra.

2

1. Linda está bien.
2. Quito está en Ecuador.
3. Paco y Ana están cansados.
4. París está en Francia.
5. Pedro está triste.

3

1. ser
2. estar
3. estar
4. estar
5. ser
6. ser
7. ser
8. estar
9. ser
10. ser

UNIDAD 5 Lección 1
Reteaching and Practice Answer Key

Did You Get it? Answer Key

4

1. estamos
2. es
3. son
4. está
5. están
6. Son
7. está
8. es

5

1. La fruta es de Florida.
2. Mis hermanos están en la cocina.
3. El perro de María es perezoso.
4. El señor Velázquez es maestro.
5. María es estudiosa.
6. Hoy es el cuatro de julio.
7. Son las tres.

6 Answers will vary.

PRÁCTICA DE GRAMÁTICA

Ordinal numbers, pp. 8–9

1

1. primer
2. noveno
3. sexto
4. tercer
5. quinto
6. séptimo
7. segundo
8. décimo
9. octavo

2

1. La primera persona lleva pantalones cortos.
2. La séptima persona lleva una chaqueta.
3. La octava persona lleva una camiseta.
4. La segunda persona lleva un vestido.
5. La tercera persona lleva un traje.
6. La quinta persona y la sexta persona llevan jeans.
7. La cuarta persona lleva una blusa.
8. La novena persona lleva un gorro.

3

1. Voy al sexto piso.
2. Voy al primer piso.
3. Voy al tercer piso.
4. Voy al décimo piso.
5. Voy al quinto piso.
6. Voy al octavo piso.
7. Voy al noveno piso.
8. Voy al cuarto piso.
9. Voy al séptimo piso.

4

1. Yo vivo en la cuarta casa de la Calle Elm.
2. El segundo libro es de Margarita.

Did You Get It? Answer Key

¿RECUERDAS?

*Stem-changing verbs **o → ue**, p. 10*

Práctica

1
1. Encuentras
2. puedo
3. dormimos
4. almorzáis
5. cuesta
6. vuelve
7. encontramos
8. Podemos
9. almuerzo
10. dormís / duermen

2 Answers will vary.

¿RECUERDAS?

Location words, p. 11

Práctica

Answers will vary.

¿RECUERDAS?

Clothing, p. 12

Práctica

1. *pantalones azules*
2. jeans negros
3. un vestido amarillo
4. una camiseta blanca
5. una blusa verde
6. gorros negros
7. una chaqueta marrón
8. pantalones cortos rojos
9. un sombrero blanco
10. zapatos anaranjados

Did You Get It? Answer Key

PRÁCTICA DE VOCABULARIO

Planning a party, pp. 14–15

❶

1. barrer el suelo
2. pasar la aspiradora
3. lavar los platos
4. cortar el césped
5. hacer la cama
6. sacar la basura
7. planchar la ropa

❷

1. Hay que lavar los platos.
2. Hay que cortar el césped.
3. Hay que sacar la basura.
4. Hay que planchar la ropa.
5. Hay que hacer la cama.
6. Hay que barrer el suelo.

❸ Hoy es el cumpleaños de Marisa. Vamos a **dar una fiesta**, pero es un secreto. Sí, ¡es una fiesta de **sorpresa**! **Los invitados** van a **venir** a las siete. Tenemos que trabajar mucho. La casa está sucia y debe estar **limpia**. Mi familia va a **ayudar**.

Mi hermano Juan va a lavar **los platos**, barrer el suelo y pasar **la aspiradora**. Mi hermana Luisa va a poner **las decoraciones**. Ella tiene **globos** de muchos colores. Mi mamá va a **cocinar** una buena comida y mi papá va a hacer el pastel. ¿Y yo? Yo voy a **envolver** los regalos para Marisa.

Cuando llega Marisa, todos vamos a **decir** «¡Sorpresa!» y «¡Feliz cumpleaños!» Vamos a **celebrar** con muchas cosas ricas y muchos platos y dulces deliciosos. También vamos a **bailar** y cantar.

❹

1. c **2.** f **3.** a
4. d **5.** b **6.** e

❺ Answers will vary.

PRÁCTICA DE GRAMÁTICA

More irregular verbs, pp. 17–18

❶ yo **digo**
los estudiantes **dicen**
vosotras **decís**
tú **dices**
Pilar **dice**

❷ vosotros **venís**
ustedes **vienen**
Rodrigo y yo **venimos**
la maestra **viene**
yo **vengo**

❸ vosotras **traéis**
tú **traes**
ellos **traen**
usted **trae**
yo **traigo**

❹ yo **pongo**
usted **pone**
Anita y yo **ponemos**
tú **pones**
usted **pone**

Did You Get It? Answer Key

5 tú **das**
ellos **dan**
yo **doy**
usted **da**
Anita y yo **damos**

6 nosotros **salimos**
ellos **salen**
yo **salgo**
usted **sale**
tú **sales**

7

1. Tú sales temprano de casa.
2. Mi hermana pone la mesa.
3. Yo pongo los globos en la sala.
4. Los invitados vienen a las siete.
5. Todos decimos/dicen «¡Feliz cumpleaños!»
6. Nosotros damos muchos regalos.

8

Ana: Félix, tú sabes que hoy **doy** una fiesta para Elena, ¿verdad? ¿Cuándo **vienes** con las decoraciones?

Félix: **Salgo** de mi casa en diez minutos. Llego en media hora.

Ana: ¿**Traes** los globos?

Félix: Sí, los llevo. Y tú, Ana, ¿qué haces?

Ana: Yo preparo la comida y **pongo** la mesa.

Félix: Y cuando **viene** Elena, todos nosotros **decimos** «¡Sorpresa!» y le **damos** los regalos.

9

1. Traigo los discos compactos.
2. Pongo las decoraciones.
3. Digo «¡Sorpresa!»
4. Doy un regalo.

PRÁCTICA DE GRAMÁTICA

Affirmative **tú** *commands, pp. 20–21*

1

1. baila
2. canta
3. cierra
4. decora
5. juega
6. llega
7. lleva
8. almuerza
9. escucha
10. celebra

2

1. aprende
2. barre
3. bebe
4. come
5. corre
6. quiere
7. trae
8. vende
9. vuelve

3

1. comparte
2. duerme
3. escribe
4. recibe
5. abre
6. vive

4

1. pon
2. haz
3. sé
4. ten
5. ve
6. sal
7. ven
8. di

UNIDAD 5 Lección 2
Reteaching and Practice Answer Key

Did You Get It? Answer Key

❺

1. Saca tus apuntes, por favor.
2. Envuelve el regalo, por favor.
3. Sirve el pastel, por favor.
4. Cierra la puerta, por favor.
5. Pon las decoraciones, por favor.
6. Llega temprano, por favor.
7. Aprende español, por favor.
8. Bebe el jugo, por favor.
9. Vende la casa, por favor.
10. Comparte el helado, por favor.

❻

1. Sí, sírvelo, por favor.
2. Sí, pídela, por favor.
3. Sí, hazlo, por favor.
4. Sí, bárrelo, por favor.
5. Sí, ponla, por favor.
6. Sí, cómpralos, por favor.
7. Sí, véndelos, por favor.
8. Sí, pásala, por favor.
9. Sí, córtalo, por favor.
10. Sí, tráelos, por favor.

¿RECUERDAS?

Tener que *and interrogative words, p. 22*

Práctica

1. Adónde
2. Por qué
3. Cuándo
4. Cúanto
5. Cómo
6. Qué

¿RECUERDAS?

Expressions of frequency, p. 23

Práctica

❶ Answers will vary.

❷ Answers will vary.

¿RECUERDAS?

Direct object pronouns, p. 24

Práctica

❶

1. *me*
2. las
3. lo
4. la
5. os
6. los
7. te
8. nos

❷

1. Sí, hazlo, por favor.
2. Sí, límpiala, por favor.
3. Sí, ponlas, por favor.
4. Sí, pásala, por favor.
5. Sí, lávalos, por favor.
6. Sí, sácala, por favor.
7. Sí, prepáralas, por favor.
8. Sí, envuélvelo, por favor.
9. Sí, córtalo, por favor.
10. Sí, tráelos, por favor.

Mi casa es su casa *Práctica de vocabulario*

Examine the floor plan of the apartment. Begin by writing the correct name of each room on the line with the corresponding number. Then, see how many Spanish words you or your partner can form from the names of the rooms. One has been done for you.

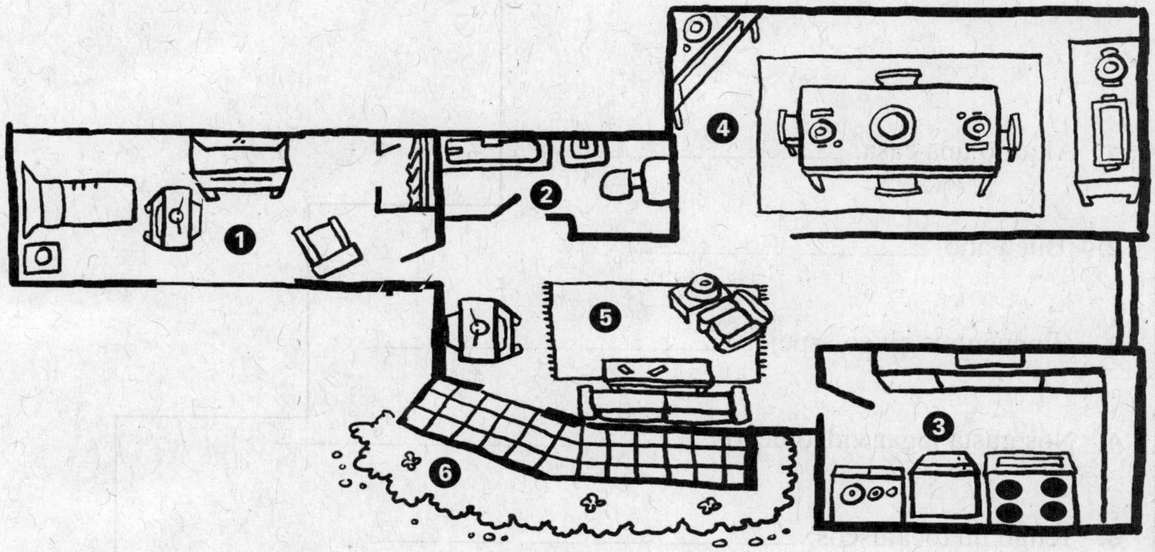

1. ______________________

2. ***baño***
   año

3. ______________________

4. ______________________

5. ______________________

6. ______________________

Nombre ____________________ Clase ______________ Fecha ______________

Cuartos escondidos *Vocabulario en contexto*

There are no ancient secrets in these hidden rooms. The name of a room or other part of a house is hidden in each of these sentences, and it's your job to find it.

1. Alquilo una casa. ___ ___ ___ ___
2. ¡Buen año! ___ ___ ___ ___
3. ¿Encuentras cinco espejos? ___ ___ ___ ___ ___
4. Nos gusta jugar videojuegos. ___ ___ ___ ___ ___ ___
5. Tengo un tocadiscos. ___ ___ ___ ___ ___ ___
6. Necesitan suelos grandes. ___ ___ ___ ___ ___ ___
7. Compro los vestidos. ___ ___ ___ ___ ___ ___ ___

Nombre ______________________ Clase ______________ Fecha ______________

Trabalenguas *Práctica de gramática 1*

Write tongue-twisting sentences that contain the verb **ser** along with words that begin with the letter *s*. Do the same for the verb **estar** and the letter *e*. Use the words in the box or come up with words of your own. The sentences can be silly, but they must use the verbs correctly. Play this game alone or with a friend, and see how many sentences you can create. If you have difficulty, you may use articles and prepositions that begin with other letters.

soy	empiezan	sincero(a)	simpático(a)	espejo	él	sillón	están	
sofá	silla	sois	sala	estoy	sirves	ella	serio(a)	somos
son	está	enojado(a)	suelo	estamos	sopa	sirvo	subir	segundo

Modelos:

SER

Sus sobrinas sesentonas (in their 60's) *son solteras* (single).

ESTAR

Efraín, el elefante, está enojado.

Nombre ______________________ Clase ______________ Fecha ______________

Ser vs. estar *Gramática en contexto*

Complete the table with the correct forms of the verbs **ser** and **estar**. Then follow the directions to spell out the answer to the riddle.

1. Si nacimos en España, __________ españoles.
2. ¿Cómo __________ vosotros?
3. ¿Mi novia? __________ alta, delgada y guapa.
4. Los maestros __________ de la Universidad de Madrid.

START (arrow pointing down to the third column)

1.									
		2.							
				3.					
		4.							

Write the letter from each step in the corresponding space below in order to figure out the hidden word.

A. Start on M
B. One step down and three steps to the right.
C. 3 steps down and 1 step to the left.
D. 3 steps to the right and 3 steps up.
E. 1 step to the left.
F. 3 steps to the left and 1 step up.
G. 4 steps down and 1 step to the right.

Una casa muy grande donde viven cantantes y actores. A nosotros nos gustaría vivir allí también. ¿Qué es?

Es una M (A) ___ (B) ___ (C) ___ (D) ___ (E) ___ (F) ___ (G).

Nombre ______________________ Clase ______________ Fecha ______________

Reunión cruzada *Práctica de gramática 2*

Carlos and Benito are meeting for the first time. After they greet each other, each asks the other where he is from, then how old he is and then what his hobbies are. At least, that's what *should* happen. Unfortunately, their conversation has gotten all mixed up! Using the ordinal numbers in the word bank, put their conversation back in order.

cuarto	décimo	noveno	octavo	primero
quinto	segundo	sexto	séptimo	tercer

1. ____________ **Carlos:** Me llamo Carlos. ¿De dónde eres?
2. ____________ **Carlos:** Yo tengo quince años. ¿Qué actividades te gusta hacer?
3. ____________ **Benito:** Necesito estudiar. Hasta luego, Carlos.
4. ____________ **Benito:** Soy de Bogotá. ¿Y tú?
5. ____________ **Benito:** Hola. Me llamo Benito. ¿Cómo te llamas?
6. ____________ **Carlos:** Me gusta leer y escribir.
7. ____________ **Carlos:** Soy de Caracas. ¿Cuántos años tienes?
8. ____________ **Carlos:** Hola.
9. ____________ **Benito:** Tengo catorce años. ¿Y cuántos años tienes tú?
10. ____________ **Benito:** Me gustan el arte y los deportes. ¿Y tú? ¿Qué te gusta hacer?

Nombre ____________ Clase ____________ Fecha ____________

Código secreto *Todo junto*

Clara wrote a note to her friend, Susana. Complete her note by cracking her code using the appropriate forms of **ser** or **estar**.

@%? ____________ **$#!** ____________

Hola Susana,

Aquí yo **@%? 1.** ____________ en mi cuarto. **@%? 2.** ____________ muy aburrida porque mi computadora **@%? 3.** ____________ en el cuarto de mi hermano. Mis padres **@%? 4.** ____________ tan ocupados que no la traen a mi cuarto. Mi hermano **@%? 5.** ____________ muy ocupado también. ¿Cómo **@%? 6.** ____________ tú? Tu hermano **$#! 7.** ____________ muy atlético, ¿sí? ¡También **$#! 8.** ____________ guapo! Pero yo **$#! 9.** ____________ joven para hablar con él. ¿Cuántos años tiene? Bueno, nosotras **$#! 10.** ____________ inteligentes y guapas también, ¿verdad (*right*)? Vamos a **$#! 11.** ____________ trabajadoras y organizadas y ¡seguro que vamos a hablar con chicos guapos! Bueno, mi madre **@%? 12.** ____________ en casa. Voy a hablar con ella sobre mi computadora.

Hasta luego, Clara

UNIDAD 5 Lección 1 Practice Games

Nombre ______________________ Clase ______________ Fecha ______________

Una casa nueva *Lectura*

Guillermo's family has just bought a new house in **Cerro Santa Ana**. His mother has asked him to make an alphabetized list of things he needs for his new room. Help Guillermo put the following objects in alphabetical order by writing the corresponding ordinal number (in the masculine singular form) next to each object.

1. **l**ámpar**a** ______________
2. cama ______________
3. **a**rma**r**io ______________
4. r**a**dio ______________
5. lec**t**or DVD ______________
6. televiso**r** ______________
7. cor**t**inas ______________
8. **es**pejo ______________
9. alfo**m**bra ______________
10. vi**d**eoju**e**gos ______________

Now write the items from Guillermo's list in alphabetical order below, making sure to circle the underlined, boldfaced letters. Then fill in the blanks below in sequential order with the letters you circled to find out when Guillermo's family is moving to their new house!

1. ______________
2. ______________
3. ______________
4. ______________
5. ______________
6. ______________
7. ______________
8. ______________
9. ______________
10. ______________

La familia de Guillermo va a su casa nueva el __ __ __ __ __ __ en __ __ __ __ __ __ __.

UNIDAD 5 Lección 1 Practice Games

Nombre _______________ Clase _______________ Fecha _______________

Tienes... *Repaso*

Figure out the five-letter word that states what your room is like. You'll find the five letters by solving the sentence puzzles. Hint: circle all the letters that the two words from **Vocabulario** have in common, then eliminate those that are also in the third word.

Mi cuarto es ____ ____ ____ ____ ____

1. This letter is in **piso** and **sillón**, but not in **otras**. ____
2. This letter is in **radio** and **comedor**, but not in **cortinas**. ____
3. This letter is in **suelo** and **ideal**, but not in **sala**. ____
4. This letter is in **cocina** and **patio**, but not in **piso**. ____
5. This letter is in **televisor** and **alfombra**, but not in **armario**. ____

Nombre ______________________ Clase ______________ Fecha ______________

Adivinanzas *Práctica de vocabulario*

Each riddle describes one of the chores from your **Volcabulario** list. Solve the riddles by stating which chores they describe.

Mi mejor (*best*) amigo tiene hambre.
Saco la comida.
Agua tiene de bebida.
¿Qué hago? ______________________

La camisa de mi madre,
Los pantalones de mi padre.
¡Qué calor! ¡Por favor!
¿Qué hago? ______________________

Una alfombra en la sala,
Una alfombra en mi cuarto.
De tanto trabajo ¡estoy harto (*fed up*)!
¿Qué hago? ______________________

Me gusta estar en el jardín.
Pero para algo (*something*) divertido,
¡no para este (*this*) trabajo tan aburrido!
¿Qué hago? ______________________

Now it's your turn to write a riddle. Describe a chore you dislike, and ask a partner to guess what the chore is. Your description does not have to rhyme, but it can if you want!

____

____

____

____

____

Nombre ______________________ Clase ______________ Fecha ______________

Preparar para la fiesta *Vocabulario en contexto*

Your family is getting ready for a big party. Your mom has put slips of paper into 10 balloons. Each balloon has a scrambled letter chore that needs to be done before the party, and one balloon has a surprise. Play this game alone or with a friend to see who gets the surprise.

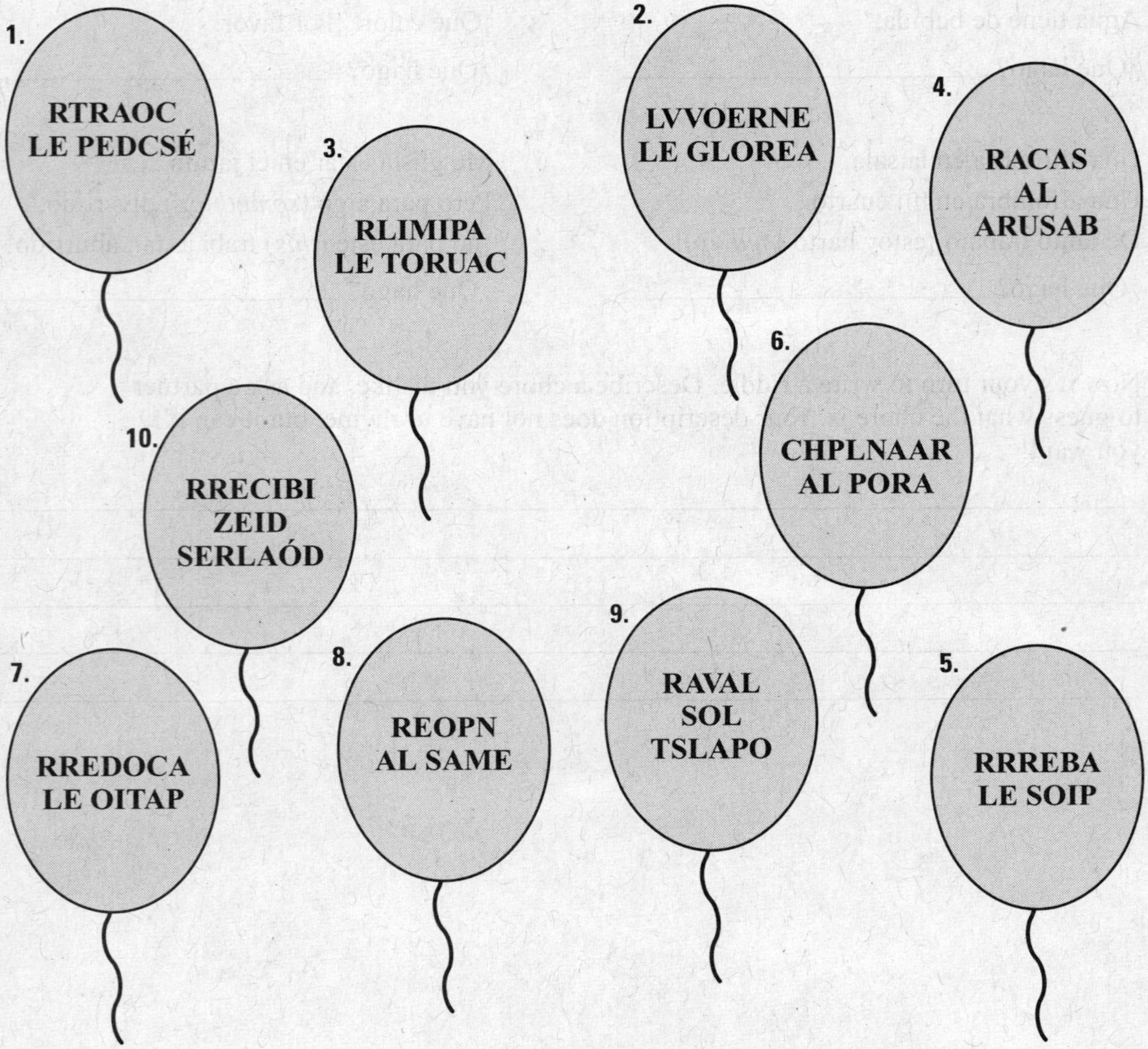

1. ______________________ 6. ______________________
2. ______________________ 7. ______________________
3. ______________________ 8. ______________________
4. ______________________ 9. ______________________
5. ______________________ 10. ______________________

UNIDAD 5 Lección 2
Practice Games

Nombre ______________________ Clase ______________ Fecha ______________

¡O... go... oy! *Práctica de gramática 1*

The **yo** forms of the following verbs follow a pattern. Fill in the blanks with the irregular **yo** form of each verb. Then use the coded numbers under the letters to complete the sentence below.

1. decir ___ ___(2) ___ ___

2. tener ___ ___ ___ ___ ___

3. venir ___ ___ ___ ___ ___(4)

4. poner ___ ___ ___ ___ ___

5. salir ___(1) ___ ___ ___ ___

6. traer ___ ___ ___ ___ ___(3) ___

7. ir ___ ___ ___

8. ser ___ ___ ___

9. dar ___ ___ ___

10. estar ___ ___ ___ ___ ___

The irregular **yo** form of the verb **seguir** is ___(1) ___(2) ___(3) ___(4) .

go oy ar

er o ir

Nombre ______________________ Clase ______________ Fecha ______________

Crucigrama *Gramática en contexto*

Use the correct form of the irregular verbs to complete the sentences and fill in the crossword puzzle.

Abajo (*down*)

1. Dolores __________ mi mejor amiga.
2. Yo __________ los platos en la mesa.
4. Yo le __________ el regalo a mi madre en su cumpleaños.
5. Yo __________ a casa en autobús todos los días.
7. Tony y Alejandro __________ tarde a la fiesta.
8. Yo __________ catorce años.

Horizontal (*across*)

3. Yo __________ de mi casa a las siete de la mañana.
4. Yo siempre __________ la verdad (*truth*) a mis padres.
5. Yo __________ a la escuela a las ocho de la mañana.
6. Enrique __________ que hoy es su cumpleaños.
8. Yo __________ mi mochila a la escuela todos los días.
9. Yo __________ cansada después de trabajar.

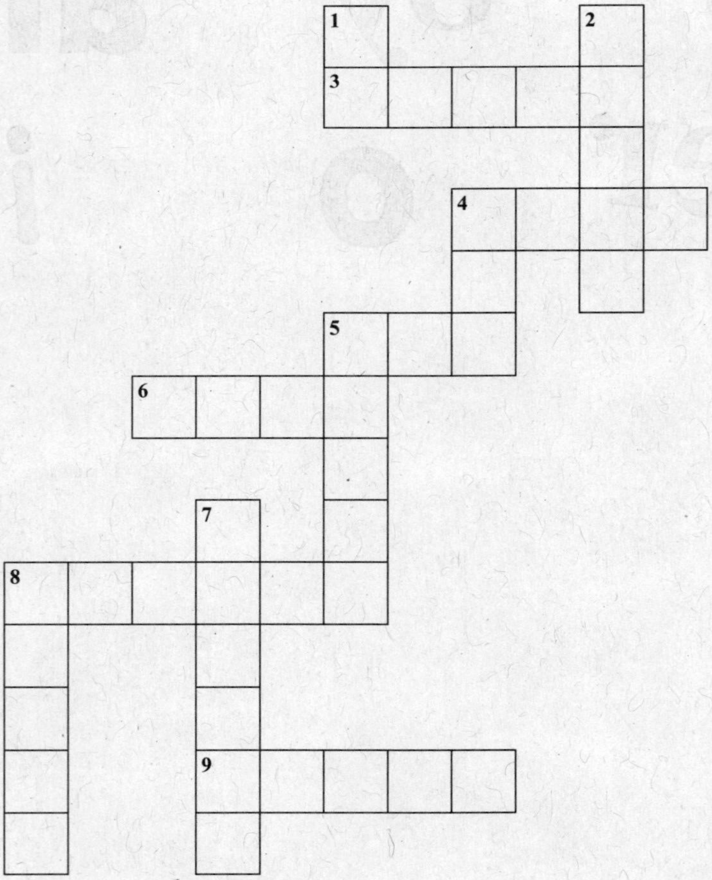

Nombre _______________ Clase _______________ Fecha _______________

Tic-Tac-Toe *Práctica de gramática 2*

By yourself or taking turns with a friend, find the forms of the affirmative tú commands in the boxes to see which letter wins at Tic-Tac-Toe. Place an **X** on the board over the correct answer for number 1. Then allow a partner to place an **O** over number 2. Play until either **X** or **O** appears three times in a row on the game board.

X	**O**
1. _____ la cama.	**2.** _____ la mesa.
3. _____ el césped.	**4.** _____ los platos.
5. _____ de comer al perro.	**6.** _____ la camisa.
7. _____ la basura.	**8.** _____ el suelo.

Pon	Barre	Corta
Dale	Haz	Saca
Lava	Plancha	Canta

Who won? _______

Nombre ______________________ Clase ______________ Fecha ______________

¡Mucho trabajo! *Todo junto*

Use the clues to fill in each line. The word formed by the circled letter will help you complete the sentence below. The first letter is provided.

Antonia está cansada después de sus ____________________ .

Q

1. _ _ _ _ _ _   _ _   _ ◯ _ _ _
2. _ _ _ ◯ _   _ _   _ _ _ _
3. _ _ _ _ _ ◯ _ _   _ _   _ _ _ _
4. _ ◯ _ _ _   _ _ _   _ _ _ _ _ _
5. ◯ _ _ _ _ _ _
6. _ _ _ ◯ _   _ _   _ _ _ _
7. _ _ _ _ ◯   _ _   _ _ _ _ _ _
8. _ _ _ _ _ _   ◯ _   _ _ _ _ _ _
9. _ _ _ _ _   _ _   _ ◯ _ _ _ _ _ _ _ _

1. El piso está sucio. Antonia necesita ____ .
2. Después de dormir, Antonia necesita ____ .
3. Después de lavar su ropa, Antonia necesita ____ .
4. Después de comer, Antonia necesita ____ .
5. Para comer la comida, Antonia necesita ____ .
6. Para comer de los platos, Antonia necesita ____ .
7. Si no quiere una casa olorosa (*smelly*), Antonia necesita ____ .
8. Antonia quiere un jardín bonito. Antonia necesita ____ .
9. Para tener una alfombra limpia, Antonia necesita ____ .

UNIDAD 5 Lección 2

Practice Games

Nombre ______________________ Clase ______________ Fecha ______________

Los invitados *Lectura cultural*

Circle the correct form of each verb. Then, write the boldfaced letters from the answers you chose in order to find out what the guests will say when Manuel arrives at the party.

1. vosotros: salir

   salís   salaís   salgaís

2. yo: poner

   pono   pongo   puso

3. yo: traer

   trayo   tralgo   traigo

4. ellos: poner

   ponan   ponen   pongan

5. él: traer

   trae   traya   traiga

6. ellos: decir

   decen   dicen   dijen

7. tú: venir

   vines   vingas   vienes

8. salir: ella

   salía   sale   sala

¡ ___ ___ ___ ___ ___ ___ ___ ___ !

UNIDAD 5 Lección 2 Practice Games

Nombre ______________________ Clase ______________ Fecha ______________

Mensajes cruzados *Repaso*

Manuel's friends are trying to keep each other up-to-date as they prepare for the party. Help them by putting together the phrases below to form correct sentences on the lines.

acaba de decorar el patio

nosotros

Elsa

Amalia y tú

Tú

acabamos de invitar a los amigos

acabáis de envolver el regalo

acabo de bailar con Jorge

acabas de recibir los globos

Yo

____

____

____

____

____

Practice Games Answer Key

PAGE 31

Práctica de vocabulario

1. cuarto: rato, arco, taco, tocar
2. baño: año
3. cocina: nací, con, cana, ni, acción
4. comedor: come, comer, me, doce
5. sala: sal, las, la, ala
6. patio: tío, pato, tapo, tipo

PAGE 32

Vocabulario en contexto

1. sala
2. baño
3. patio
4. jardín
5. cocina
6. cuarto
7. comedor

PAGE 33

Práctica de gramática 1

Answer will vary. Possible answers: Soy Susana Silva de San Sebastián; Somos secretarias simpáticas; Elena está enferma; El elefante enorme está en Ecuador.

PAGE 34

Gramática en contexto

START

1. S	O	M	O	S					
		2. E	S	T	A	I	S		
				3. E	S				
		4. S	O	N					

Answer to riddle: MANSIÓN

UNIDAD 5 Lección 1 Practice Games Answer Key

Practice Games Answer Key

PAGE 35

Práctica de gramática 2

Reunión cruzada

1. tercero
2. séptimo
3. décimo
4. cuarto
5. segundo
6. noveno
7. quinto
8. primero
9. sexto
10. octavo

PAGE 36

Todo junto

estoy, Estoy, está, están, está, estás, es, es, soy, somos, ser, está

PAGE 37

Lectura

1. sexto
2. tercero
3. segundo
4. octavo
5. séptimo
6. noveno
7. cuarto
8. quinto
9. primero
10. décimo

1. alfo**m**bra
2. **a**rma**r**io
3. cama
4. cor**t**inas
5. **es**pejo
6. **l**ámpar**a**
7. lec**t**or DVD
8. r**a**dio
9. televiso**r**
10. vi**d**eoju**e**gos

La familia de Guillermo va a su casa nueva el **martes** en **la tarde**.

PAGE 38

Repaso de la lección

I-D-E-A-L

Practice Games Answer Key

PAGE 39

Práctica de vocabulario

darle de comer al perro
pasar la aspiradora
planchar la ropa
cortar el césped

Answers will vary, but should describe a chore without naming it.

PAGE 40

Vocabulario en contexto

1. cortar el césped
2. envolver el regalo
3. limpiar el cuarto
4. sacar la basura
5. barrer el piso
6. planchar la ropa
7. decorar el patio
8. poner la mesa
9. lavar los platos
10. recibir diez dólares

PAGE 41

Práctica de gramática 1

1. digo
2. tengo
3. vengo
4. pongo
5. salgo
6. traigo
7. voy
8. soy
9. doy
10. estoy

sigo

PAGE 42

Gramática en contexto

Vertical	Horizontal
1. pongo	**1.** salgo
2. doy	**2.** digo
3. vengo	**3.** voy
4. vienen	**4.** traigo
5. es	**5.** dice
6. tengo	**6.** estoy

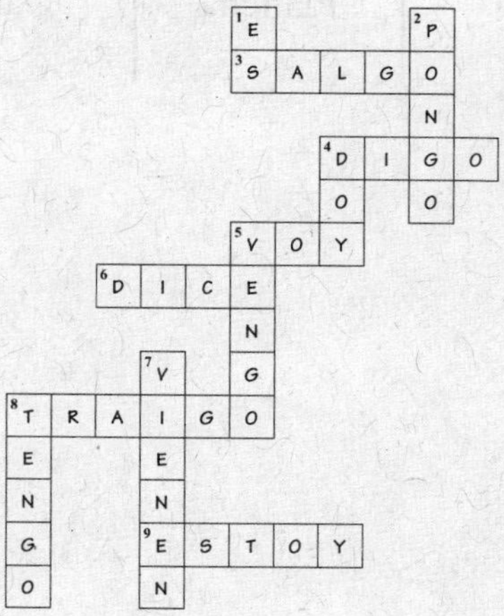

Practice Games Answer Key

PAGE 43

Práctica de gramática 2

O Pon	*O* Barre	X Corta
X Dale	X Haz	X Saca
O Lava	*O* Plancha	Canta

X wins.

PAGE 44

Todo junto

Antonia está cansada después de sus QUEHACERES

1. Barrer el sUelo
2. hacEr la cama
3. plancHar la ropa
4. lAvar los platos
5. Cocinar
6. ponEr la mesa
7. sacarR la basura
8. cortar el céspEd
9. pasar la aSpiradora

PAGE 45

Lectura cultural

1. salís
2. pongo
3. traigo
4. ponen
5. trae
6. dicen
7. vienes
8. sale

"sorpresa"

PAGE 46

Repaso de la lección

Elsa acaba de decorar el patio.
Amalia y tú acabáis de envolver el regalo.
Nosotros acabamos de invitar a los amigos.
Tú acabas de recibir los globos.
Yo acabo de bailar con Jorge.

Nombre ______________________ Clase ______________ Fecha ______________

Video Activities *Vocabulario*

PRE-VIEWING ACTIVITY

1. What are the most important rooms in your house?

____

____

2. Choose one room in your house or apartment and describe it in detail. Where is it? What furniture and other items are in it?

____

____

3. Describe your ideal house.

____

____

4. Choose one room of your ideal house and describe it in detail.

____

____

VIEWING ACTIVITY

Read the list of items below before you watch the video. While you watch, write E if the item is something Elena wants in her house. Write F if Fernando wants it in his apartment.

1. _____ Una alfombra en el cuarto

2. _____ Una cama grande

3. _____ Cortinas azules

4. _____ Discos compactos

5. _____ Una mesa en la sala

6. _____ Muebles bonitos

7. _____ Un sillón en la sala

8. _____ Un televisor

Nombre ______________________ Clase ______________ Fecha ______________

Video Activities *Vocabulario*

POST-VIEWING ACTIVITY

Choose the item that best completes the sentence.

1. En la casa ideal de Elena, hay un cuarto que tiene una __________ .

a. cama

b. mesa

c. cocina

2. Fernando quiere sentarse en un __________ grande.

a. sofá

b. espejo

c. alfombra

3. Elena quiere mirar en un __________ .

a. sillón

b. espejo

c. televisor

4. Fernando quiere mirar al __________ .

a. sillón

b. espejo

c. televisor

5. Elena quiere unas __________ azules.

a. sillas

b. cortinas

c. alfombras

Nombre ______________________ Clase ______________ Fecha ______________

Video Activities *Telehistoria escena 1*

PRE-VIEWING ACTIVITY

Answer the following questions about studying.

1. How much time do you usually spend studying for an important test?
____
2. Where do you usually study?
____
3. How often do you study with classmates or friends?
____
4. What is an advantage to studying in groups?
____

VIEWING ACTIVITY

Read this activity before watching the video. Then, while watching the video, match each activity below with the place where Manuel prefers to do it. Hint: There are places in this activity that he does not prefer for any of the activities. He prefers others for more than one activity.

a.

b.

c.

d.

1. _____ escuchar discos compactos

2. _____ jugar videojuegos

3. _____ estudiar

Nombre ______________________ Clase ______________ Fecha ______________

Video Activities *Telehistoria escena 1*

POST-VIEWING ACTIVITY

Indicate whether each of the following statements is True (T) or False (F).

1. La señora Cuevas habla con Fernando en el jardín de su casa. T F
2. La señora Cuevas piensa que Manuel escucha discos compactos en su cuarto. T F
3. Manuel y Elena están en la cocina cuando llega Fernando. T F
4. Manuel y Fernando van al cuarto de Manuel a estudiar. T F
5. A Elena no le gusta jugar a los videojuegos. T F

Nombre ______________________ Clase ______________ Fecha ______________

Video Activities *Telehistoria escena 2*

PRE-VIEWING ACTIVITY

Answer the following questions.

1. What chores do you have to do at home?
____

2. How often do you have to do each chore?
____
____
____

3. Which chore do you find the most pleasant?
____

4. Which chore do you dread the most?
____

VIEWING ACTIVITY

Manuel is looking for two things in the video. Read the following two sentences before watching the video. Then, while watching the video, complete each sentence with the correct place in which each item is found.

1. El cuaderno de Manuel está ____________

a. cerca de la lámpara.

b. en el armario.

c. en el suelo.

d. en la cómoda.

e. encima de la cama.

2. La camiseta de Alicia está ____________

a. en la cocina.

b. en la sala.

c. en el cuarto de Manuel.

d. en la escalera.

e. en el comedor.

Nombre ______________________ Clase ______________ Fecha ______________

Video Activities *Telehistoria escena 2*

POST-VIEWING ACTIVITY

Choose the word that best completes each of the following sentences.

sillón	**cama**	**ocupado**	**cuarto**	**desorganizado**	**suelo**	**centro**

1. Muchas de las cosas de Manuel están en el ________________.

2. Manuel encuentra su cuaderno al lado de la ________________.

3. Manuel es ________________.

4. Manuel y Fernando estudian en el ________________ de Manuel.

5. La camiseta de Alicia está al lado del ________________.

6. Manuel está ________________ ahora.

7. Fernando y Manuel van a ver a Trini Salgado en el ________________ de Quito.

Nombre ______________________ Clase ______________ Fecha ______________

Video Activities *Telehistoria escena 3*

PRE-VIEWING ACTIVITY

Answer the following questions.

1. Do you misplace things often?

   ____

2. What types of things do you usually misplace?

   ____

3. Where is the most unusual place that you've found a misplaced item?

   ____

4. In your opinion, what is the best thing to do if you misplace something?

   ____

VIEWING ACTIVITY

Read through the list of locations below before watching the video. Then, while watching the video, indicate with a checkmark (✓) if the location is a place Manuel looks for Alicia's T-shirt in the video.

__________ en el jardín

__________ en las cortinas

__________ en la mesa

__________ en la planta baja de la casa

__________ en el patio

__________ en el sofá

__________ en el comedor

__________ en la cocina

__________ en el segundo piso

Nombre _______________ Clase _______________ Fecha _______________

Video Activities *Telehistoria escena 3*

POST-VIEWING ACTIVITY

Put the following events in the correct order.

_______ Manuel va al comedor y la camiseta no está allí.

_______ La señora Cuevas no quiere hablar con Manuel.

_______ Fernando ve el gato de Elena y está encima de una camiseta.

_______ Manuel y Fernando bajan las escaleras.

_______ Manuel va a la cocina y la camiseta no está allí.

_______ Manuel va al jardín.

_______ La camiseta que está debajo del gato es la camiseta de Alicia.

Nombre ____________________ Clase ______________ Fecha ______________

Video Activities *Vocabulario*

PRE-VIEWING ACTIVITY

1. Think about a party you have attended. What was the party celebrating?

   ____

2. What decorations were there?

   ____

3. What activities took place at the party?

   ____

4. What do you think the hosts had to do to prepare their house?

   ____

VIEWING ACTIVITY

Read the chores below before you watch the movie. While you watch, put a check (✓) next to each chore that the characters do in the afternoon before Manuel's surprise party.

______ Barrer el suelo

______ Cocinar la comida

______ Comprar los regalos

______ Hacer las camas

______ Lavar el auto

______ Lavar los platos

______ Pintar la casa

______ Poner los globos

______ Sacar la basura

Nombre ______________________ Clase ______________ Fecha ______________

Video Activities *Vocabulario*

POST-VIEWING ACTIVITY

Choose the word from the word bank that best completes each sentence.

barre	**invitados**	**platos**	**poner**	**sorpresa**	**quehaceres**	**saca**

1. Manuel no sabe de la fiesta porque es una ______________.

2. Los ______________ son todos sus amigos.

3. Antes de la fiesta, los amigos de Manuel necesitan cumplir los ______________.

4. Fernando va a ______________ los globos.

5. El papá de Elena ______________ el suelo.

6. Necesitan lavar los ______________ antes de comer.

7. Elena ______________ la basura porque quiere una casa limpia.

Nombre ______________________ Clase ______________ Fecha ______________

Video Activities *Telehistoria escena 1*

PRE-VIEWING ACTIVITY

Imagine you are throwing a birthday party for a friend at your house. Answer the following questions about how you will prepare for the event.

1. Write a shopping list of the foods and decorations that you need to buy.

____

____

2. What are some chores you need to do to prepare your house for the party? List at least five.

____

____

3. What else do you need to do to prepare for the party?

____

____

VIEWING ACTIVITY

Read the sentences below before watching the video. Then, while watching the video, match the appropriate person with each activity. Hint: One person does more than one activity.

1. _____ Pone la mesa.

2. _____ Hablan del regalo para Manuel.

3. _____ Decora la casa.

4. _____ Pregunta dónde está Manuel.

5. _____ Hablan y beben ponche *(punch)*.

6. _____ Quiere ayudar en la cocina.

a. señora Cuevas

b. señor Cuevas

c. Fernando

d. los invitados

e. Fernando y Elena

Nombre ______________________ Clase ______________________ Fecha ______________________

Video Activities *Telehistoria escena 1*

POST-VIEWING ACTIVITY

Choose the word that best completes each of the following sentences.

cocina	**invitados**	**fiesta**	**regalo**	**puerta**	**mesa**

1. Los regalos están en la ______________________ .

2. El ______________________ que trae Fernando es un videojuego.

3. Hay muchos ______________________ en la fiesta.

4. Fernando no quiere abrir la ______________________ a los invitados.

5. Fernando va a ayudar en la ______________________ .

6. Manuel va a venir a la ______________________ .

Video Activities *Telehistoria escena 2*

PRE-VIEWING ACTIVITY

Answer the following questions.

1. Have you ever thrown or been to a surprise party? Whose party was it?

   ____

2. What are some things you can do to keep a surprise party a secret? List three things.

   ____

   ____

   ____

3. Has anyone ever thrown a surprise party for you? What was the occasion?

   ____

4. Have you or someone you know found out early about a party that was meant to be a surprise? What ruined the secret?

   ____

VIEWING ACTIVITY

Read the following statements before watching the video. Then, while watching the video, indicate whether each statement is True (T) or False (F).

1.	Hay muchos coches enfrente de la casa de Manuel.	T	F
2.	Manuel está emocionado porque tiene el autógrafo de Trini Salgado.	T	F
3.	Manuel ve un globo marrón.	T	F
4.	Todos dicen "¡Feliz cumpleaños!".	T	F
5.	Elena tiene el pastel de cumpleaños.	T	F
6.	A Manuel le gusta mucho el regalo de Fernando.	T	F
7.	Los padres de Manuel no quieren bailar.	T	F
8.	Los invitados no tienen ganas de bailar.	T	F

Nombre ______________________ Clase ______________ Fecha ______________

Video Activities *Telehistoria escena 2*

POST-VIEWING ACTIVITY

Put the following events in the correct order.

_________ Fernando pone los regalos en una silla.

_________ Manuel viene de Quito con la camiseta de Alicia.

_________ Elena trae el pastel de cumpleaños.

_________ Los padres de Manuel bailan.

_________ Los invitados dicen "¡Sorpresa!" a Manuel.

_________ Manuel abre todos sus regalos.

_________ Manuel ve un globo detrás de la casa.

Nombre ______________________ Clase ______________ Fecha ______________

Video Activities *Telehistoria escena 3*

PRE-VIEWING ACTIVITY

Answer the following questions.

1. What are the daily chores that have to be done at your house?

____

____

2. What are the weekly chores at your house?

____

____

3. Are the chores at your house assigned by a certain person or do you get to choose what you have to do?

____

4. What chores need to be done after a party? List four.

____

____

VIEWING ACTIVITY

Read the phrases below before watching the video. Then complete the activity as you watch. Write **sí** *(yes)* next to the statements that that are said to Elena and **no** *(no)* next to the statements that are not said to Elena.

1. ________ Pon los platos en la cocina.
2. ________ Barre el suelo y saca la basura.
3. ________ Lava la ropa.
4. ________ Manuel tiene que ayudar con los quehaceres.
5. ________ ¡Ahora no voy a ayudar!
6. ________ Acabo de lavar la ropa.

Nombre ____________________ Clase ______________ Fecha ______________

Video Activities *Telehistoria escena 3*

POST-VIEWING ACTIVITY

Choose the word or phrase that best completes each of the following sentences.

1. Elena tiene que barrer el suelo y __________ .

a. lavar los platos

b. pasar la aspiradora

c. sacar la basura

2. Manuel no quiere ayudar porque busca __________ .

a. la camiseta

b. el videojuego

c. el autógrafo de Trini Salgado

3. Manuel no tiene que limpiar porque es __________ .

a. el sábado

b. el viernes

c. su cumpleaños

4. El señor Cuevas __________ la ropa.

a. lava

b. plancha

c. hace

5. La camiseta de Alicia ya no está __________ .

a. limpia

b. sucia

c. azul

Video Activities Answer Key

VOCABULARIO pp. 51–52

PRE-VIEWING ACTIVITY

1. Answers will vary. Possible answer: The most important rooms in my house are the living room, the kitchen and my bedroom.
2. Answers will vary. Possible answer: My bedroom is on the second floor. It has a bed, a desk, a chair and a dresser.
3. Answers will vary. Possible answer: My ideal house is much bigger than the one I have. I have my own room, instead of sharing with my brother, and we all have our own bathrooms. The house even has a pool.
4. Answers will vary. Possible answer: When I enter my ideal house, the first room I see is the living room. It is a large, comfortable room with a blue rug. It has a big sofa and two soft chairs.

VIEWING ACTIVITY

1. E
2. E
3. E
4. F
5. F
6. E
7. E
8. F

POST-VIEWING ACTIVITY

1. a
2. a
3. b
4. c
5. b

TELEHISTORIA ESCENA 1 pp. 53–54

PRE-VIEWING ACTIVITY

1. Answers will vary. Possible answer: I usually study for about an hour and a half for an important test.
2. Answers will vary. Possible answer: I usually study at home in my room.
3. Answers will vary. Possible answer: I usually study in groups about once each month.
4. Answers will vary. Possible answer: It is often easier to remember something you have discussed with a friend.

VIEWING ACTIVITY

1. c
2. b
3. c

POST-VIEWING ACTIVITY

1. T
2. T
3. F
4. T
5. F

TELEHISTORIA ESCENA 2 pp. 55–56

PRE-VIEWING ACTIVITY

1. Answers will vary. Possible answer: I have to take out the trash, do the dishes after supper and keep my room clean.
2. Answers will vary. Possible answer: I take out the trash once a week. I do the dishes every evening. I always keep my room tidy.
3. Answers will vary. Possible answer: I like doing the dishes.
4. Answers will vary. Possible answer: Taking out the garbage is my least favorite chore.

VIEWING ACTIVITY

1. c
2. b

POST-VIEWING ACTIVITY

1. suelo
2. cama
3. desorganizado
4. cuarto
5. sillón
6. ocupado
7. centro

TELEHISTORIA ESCENA 3 pp. 57–58

PRE-VIEWING ACTIVITY

1. Answers will vary. Possible answer: Yes, I misplace things often.
2. Answers will vary. Possible answer: I usually misplace my backpack and my glasses.
3. Answers will vary. Possible answer: I found my glasses in the refrigerator!
4. Answers will vary. Possible answer: When I lose something, I try to remember the last thing I did when I had the item.

VIEWING ACTIVITY

Marked item should be: en el jardín; en la mesa; en la planta baja de la casa; en el comedor; en la cocina

POST-VIEWING ACTIVITY

Manuel va al comedor y la camiseta no está allí. **4**

La señora Cuevas no quiere hablar con Manuel. **3**

Fernando ve el gato de Elena y está encima de una camiseta. **6**

Manuel y Fernando bajan las escaleras. **1**

Manuel va a la cocina y la camiseta no está allí. **5**

Manuel va al jardín. **2**

La camiseta que está debajo del gato es la camiseta de Alicia. **7**

Video Activities Answer Key

VOCABULARIO pp. 59–60

PRE-VIEWING ACTIVITY

1. Answers will vary. Possible answer: The party was for Halloween.
2. Answers will vary. Possible answer: There were orange and black streamers and balloons.
3. Answers will vary. Possible answer: We played games, ate and danced to music.
4. Answers will vary. Possible answer: They probably vacuumed or swept and washed the dishes.

VIEWING ACTIVITY

Marked items should be: Barrer el suelo; Hacer las camas; Lavar las platos; Poner los globos; Sacar la basura

POST-VIEWING ACTIVITY

1. sorpresa
2. invitados
3. quehaceres
4. poner
5. barre
6. platos
7. saca

TELEHISTORIA ESCENA 1 pp. 61–62

PRE-VIEWING ACTIVITY

1. Answers will vary. Possible answer: Foods: frozen pizza, chips, salsa, candy, soda, fruit punch, a birthday cake, ice cream, hamburger patties and buns. Decorations: balloons, streamers, candles and confetti
2. Answers will vary. Possible answer: I need to clean the kitchen, vacuum the living room, dust the furniture, mop the kitchen floor and cut the grass in the yard.
3. Answers will vary. Possible answer: I need to buy a present for my friend and wrap it. I also need to mix a CD for the party.

VIEWING ACTIVITY

1. a	2. e
3. b	4. a
5. d	6. c

POST-VIEWING ACTIVITY

1. mesa
2. regalo
3. invitados
4. puerta
5. cocina
6. fiesta

TELEHISTORIA ESCENA 2 pp. 63–64

PRE-VIEWING ACTIVITY

1. Answers will vary. Possible answer: Yes, I have thrown a surprise birthday party for a friend who was moving away.
2. Answers will vary. Possible answer: You can invite a small number of people to the party and tell them to keep the secret. You can pretend that you forgot that it was your friend's birthday. You can pretend to have other plans the night of the party.
3. Answers will vary. Possible answer: Yes, I had a surprise party for my eleventh birthday.
4. Answers will vary. Possible answer: My younger brother told me about the surprise party for my birthday.

VIEWING ACTIVITY

1. T	2. T
3. F	4. F
5. T	6. T
7. F	8. T

POST-VIEWING ACTIVITY

Fernando pone los regalos en una silla. 5

Manuel viene de Quito con la camiseta de Alicia. 1

Elena trae el pastel de cumpleaños. 4

Los padres de Manuel bailan. 7

Los invitados dicen «¡Sorpresa!» a Manuel. 3

Manuel abre todos sus regalos. 6

Manuel ve un globo detrás de la casa. 2

TELEHISTORIA ESCENA 3 pp. 65–66

PRE-VIEWING ACTIVITY

1. Answers will vary. Possible answer: The dishes are done at my house after every meal and I have to keep my room clean. I make my bed every morning, and I also have to feed our dog Buster twice a day.
2. Answers will vary. Possible answer: Every week the trash gets taken out, I clean the bathroom, the furniture gets dusted and the carpet in the living room gets vacuumed.
3. Answers will vary. Possible answer: My mother writes a list of everything that has to be done and who has to do each chore.
4. Answers will vary. Possible answer: After a party the carpet needs to be vacuumed, the floors need to be mopped, the dishes need to be washed and the trash needs to be picked up and taken out.

VIEWING ACTIVITY

1. no	2. sí
3. no	4. no
5. sí	6. sí

POST-VIEWING ACTIVITY

1. c	2. a
3. c	4. a
5. b	

Video Scripts

VOCABULARIO

Elena: Fernando, ¡que casa!

Fernando: Tiene un jardín muy bonito.

Elena: ¡Es mi casa ideal!

Fernando: ¿Sí, Elena? ¿Y cómo es tu casa ideal?

Elena: Hmmm.... en la planta baja, están la sala el comedor, la cocina. En la sala hay un sillón. ¡Mis muebles son muy bonitos!

Fernando: ¡Tu casa es muy grande!

Elena: Subimos al segundo piso. Allí están los cuartos.

Fernando: ¿Y no tiene un patio?

Elena: No, no me gusta mucho.

Fernando: ¿Y cómo es tu cuarto?

Elena: Mi cuarto tiene una cama grande, una cómoda, unas cortinas de color azul, una alfombra y un espejo...

Fernando: ¡Pues! ¡Que casa! Mi casa ideal es un poco diferente.

Elena: ¿Ah, sí? ¿Cómo es?

Fernando: No es una casa, es un apartamento. Está en el quinto piso. En la sala hay un sofá, un televisor, una mesa donde tengo mi radio, mi tocadiscos compactos, mis videojuegos y mis discos compactos.

Elena: Tu casa ideal, ¿eh?

TELEHISTORIA ESCENA 1

Fernando: ¿Cómo está, señora Cuevas?

Madre: ¿Qué tal, Fernando?

Fernando: ¿Está Manuel?

Madre: Sí, escucha discos compactos en su cuarto.

Fernando: Ah, gracias. Voy a subir.

Madre: O está en la sala. Le gusta mucho jugar videojuegos con Elena. ¿Van a estudiar?

Fernando: Sí.

Madre: Bueno. ¡Ah! Fernando. Es para Manuel.

Fernando: Hola.

Manuel: Hola, Fernando.

Elena: Hola, Fernando. ¿Van a estudiar aquí en la sala, en el comedor o en el cuarto de Manuel?

Fernando: ¿Manuel?

Elena: ¡Manuel!

Manuel: ¡OK! ¿Qué tal si estudiamos en mi cuarto?

Video Scripts

TELEHISTORIA ESCENA 2

Manuel: ¡Mi cuaderno no está aquí!

Fernando: ¿Encima de la cama?

Manuel: No.

Fernando: Y, ¿cerca de la lámpara?

Manuel: No.

Fernando: ¿En el armario?

Manuel: No.

Fernando: ¿En la cómoda?

Manuel: No.

Fernando: Manuel, ¡eres muy desorganizado! ¡Todas tus cosas están en el suelo!

Elena: ¡Manuel! ¡Manuel!

Manuel: ¿Qué quieres? Estoy muy ocupado.

Elena: Sí, tú eres muy estudioso.

Fernando: ¿Tienes que ir al centro de Quito? ¿A ver a Trini Salgado?

Manuel: Sí. ¡Alicia quiere el autógrafo de Trini! Es importante. Tenemos que ir.

Fernando: Manuel. ¿Y la camiseta?

TELEHISTORIA ESCENA 3

Manuel: ¡Mamá! ¡Mamá! ¡La camiseta! ¿Dónde está?

Madre: ¿Qué camiseta?

Manuel: La camiseta de Alicia, mi amiga de Miami.

Madre: Ay, hijo. Aquí, en el jardín, no está. Tiene que estar en la casa.

Manuel: ¡Mamá! Por favor.

Madre: Manuel, estoy ocupada.

Manuel: ¿Dónde está? Aquí, en la mesa, no está.

Fernando: Hmm, no está encima de la mesa. No está en tu cuarto.

Manuel: No. ¡Tiene que estar aquí, en la planta baja!

Fernando: ¿En el comedor, en la cocina? Hmmm, Manuel... Aquí hay un gato, al lado del sillón.

Manuel: Sí, es Fígaro, el gato de Elena. ¿Y qué?

Fernando: El gato está encima de una camiseta. Ay, Manuel, eres muy desorganizado.

Video Scripts

VOCABULARIO

Madre: Vamos a celebrar el cumpleaños de Manuel.

Elena: Vamos a dar una fiesta en casa.

Madre: Es una fiesta sorpresa. Es un secreto, ¿eh?

All: ¡Sorpresa!

Elena: Hay que trabajar mucho. Fernando, ¿Puedes ayudar?

Fernando: ¿Con qué? ¿Con las decoraciones? Yo voy a poner los globos.

Elena: Mamá, ¿vas a bailar con papá?

Madre: Y tú, Elena, ¿vas a cantar?

Fernando: Y, ¿quiénes son los invitados?

Elena: Debes invitar a todos los amigos.

Madre: Pero primero los quehaceres: barrer el suelo, cortar el césped, pasar la aspiradora, hacer las camas.

Elena: ¡Acabo de hacer la cama!

Madre: Sacar la basura, lavar los platos... Ahora sí, la casa está limpia. ¡Debemos envolver los regalos! Elena, ¿puedes buscar el papel de regalo?

TELEHISTORIA ESCENA 1

Fernando: ¿Y los regalos? ¿Dónde?

Madre: En la mesa.

Elena: Fernando, ¿qué regalo traes para Manuel?

Fernando: Un videojuego. Lo acabo de envolver.

Padre: Un videojuego. ¡Qué sorpresa!

Fernando: ¿Puedo ayudar?

Elena: Sí, puedes abrir la puerta a los invitados.

Fernando: Ay, prefiero preparar la comida. ¡Me gusta cocinar!

Padre: Bueno, puedes ayudar en la cocina.

Guest 1: ¿Dónde está Manuel?

Guest 2: No sé.

Madre: ¿Qué hora es? ¿Dónde está tu hermano?

Fernando: Acabo de hablar por teléfono con Manuel. Va a venir.

All: ¡Qué alegría! ¡Qué bien!

TELEHISTORIA ESCENA 2

Fernando: ¡El autógrafo de Trini!

Elena: ¡Allí viene Manuel!

All: ¡Sorpresa!

Madre: ¡Feliz cumpleaños, hijo!

Padre: ¡Feliz cumpleaños!

Elena: ¡Feliz cumpleaños! ¡Aquí viene el pastel!

All: ¡Bravo!

Manuel: Y... ¿qué hago ahora?

Fernando: ¡Abrir los regalos! Yo los traigo. Yo los pongo aquí.

Manuel: ¡Qué sorpresa! ¡Un videojuego! No lo tengo. Muchas gracias, Fernando... Gracias.

Fernando: Hmmm... ¿Y qué hacemos ahora?

Padre: ¡A bailar todos!

Video Scripts

TELEHISTORIA ESCENA 3

Madre: Pon los platos sucios allí. Ponlos con la ropa sucia.

Padre: Elena, barre el suelo, saca la basura, y yo lavo la ropa.

Elena: ¿Y Manuel? ¿Por qué no ayuda?

Madre: Acaba de celebrar su cumpleaños. Hoy no tiene que limpiar...

Elena: ¿Vienes a ayudar? Toma...

Manuel: ¡Elenaaa! Ahora ¡no! Tengo que buscar la camiseta de Alicia. ¿Dónde está? ¿Mamá?

Manuel: ¿Papá?

Padre: ¿Sí?

Elena: La camiseta de Alicia, ¿dónde está?

Padre: ¡Ay! ¡Acabo de lavarla!

COMPARACIÓN CULTURAL VIDEO

Throughout the Spanish-speaking world, you can see some very different styles of houses. Here we are going to show you residential areas in Ecuador, a very interesting neighborhood in the Dominican Republic and a museum in Spain that used to be the home of an artist.

Ecuador
This is the city of Quito, in Ecuador, a city 9,186 feet above sea level, surrounded by mountains and volcanoes.

During the Spanish colonial period, churches, banks and plazas were built with mud, stone, brick and wood. Today, these places are part of the Historic "Old City" of Quito.

Although there are people who live in the Old City, most of Quito has become a modern city, with modern apartment buildings.

Dominican Republic
This is the neighborhood of Gazcue in Santo Domingo, the Dominican Republic. It is a formerly exclusive residential area with houses of unique architecture from the 1940s and 50s. The houses in Gazcue are very different from one another, and contain architectural details that enhance the neighborhood.

Spain
Some houses are very important to the history of a country. This one in Toledo, Spain, was home to the famous painter, El Greco. Today, it is a museum. More than 20 of the best known paintings of El Greco call this museum "home."

Here we saw the old and new Quito in Ecuador, visited Gazcue in the Dominican Republic, and learned about El Greco's house and museum in Spain. Can you think of any distinctive homes in your neighborhood or in your city?

Audio Scripts

UNIDAD 5, LECCIÓN 1
TEXTBOOK SCRIPTS
TXT CD 5

PRESENTACIÓN DE VOCABULARIO

Level 1 Textbook pp. 248–249

Level 1B Textbook pp. 42–44

TXT CD 5, Track 1

A. ¡Hola! Me llamo Manuel. Vivo en una casa grande. Tiene dos pisos. Hay un patio y un jardín detrás de la casa.

B. A Elena y a mí nos gusta jugar videojuegos en la sala. En la cocina preparamos la comida y en el comedor comemos todos los días.

C. Cuando subimos la escalera, llegamos a mi cuarto. Allí me gusta estudiar, escuchar mis discos compactos y descansar.

D. En mi cuarto tengo un tocadiscos compactos, un radio y otras cosas.

E. Mi amigo Fernando piensa que vivir en un apartamento es ideal. Prefiere vivir en un apartamento donde puede ver el centro de Quito.

¡A RESPONDER!

Level 1 Textbook p. 249

TXT CD 5, Track 2

Level 1B Textbook p. 44

Level 1B TXT CD, Track 6

Escucha la lista de las cosas que hay en la casa. Indica la foto del cuarto donde se encuentra cada cosa.

1. Hay una alfombra.
2. Hay una cómoda.
3. Hay una lámpara.
4. Hay un espejo.
5. Hay un sillón.
6. Hay una cama.
7. Hay un sofá.
8. Hay unas cortinas.

TELEHISTORIA ESCENA 1

Level 1 Textbook p. 251

Level 1B Textbook p. 46

TXT CD 5, Track 3

Fernando: ¿Cómo está, señora Cuevas? ¿Está Manuel?

Sra. Cuevas: ¿Qué tal, Fernando? Sí, escucha discos compactos en su cuarto...

Fernando: Ah, gracias. Voy a subir.

Sra. Cuevas: ...o está en la sala. Le gusta mucho jugar videojuegos con Elena. ¿Van a estudiar?

Fernando: Sí.

Sra. Cuevas: Bueno. ¡Ah! Fernando, es para Manuel.

Fernando: Hola.

Manuel: Hola, Fernando.

Elena: Hola, Fernando. ¿Van a estudiar aquí en la sala, en el comedor o en el cuarto de Manuel?

Fernando: ¿Manuel?

Elena: ¡Manuel!

Manuel: ¡OK! ¿Qué tal si estudiamos en mi cuarto?

ACTIVIDAD 8 – LOS AMIGOS DE MANUEL

Level 1 Textbook p. 254

TXT CD 5, Track 4

Level 1B Textbook p. 49

Level 1B TXT CD, Track 7

Manuel describe a varias personas. Escucha su descripción y toma apuntes. Contesta las preguntas.

Estoy contento hoy porque voy a hablar por teléfono con mis amigos. Mi amiga Rosa es de Chile. Es cómica y muy inteligente. Su casa está cerca del centro comercial. Mis amigos José y Carlos son de Estados Unidos. Son altos y cómicos. Son hermanos. Su apartamento está cerca de la escuela. Es grande y muy bonito.

TELEHISTORIA ESCENA 2

Level 1 Textbook p. 256

Level 1B Textbook p. 52

TXT CD 5, Track 5

Manuel: ¡Mi cuaderno no está aquí!

Fernando: Y, ¿encima de la cama? ¿Y cerca de la lámpara? ¿Y en el armario? ¿En la cómoda?

Fernando: Manuel, ¡eres muy desorganizado! ¡Todas tus cosas están en el suelo!

Elena: ¡Manuel! ¡Manueeeel!

Manuel: ¿Qué quieres? Estoy muy ocupado.

Elena: Sí, tú eres muy estudioso.

Fernando: ¿Tienes que ir al centro de Quito? ¿A ver a Trini Salgado?

Manuel: Sí. ¡Alicia quiere el autógrafo de Trini! Es importante. Tenemos que ir.

Fernando: Manuel… ¿y la camiseta?

PRONUNCIACIÓN
La acentuación

Level 1 Textbook p. 259

Level 1B Textbook p. 56

TXT CD 5, Track 6

In Spanish, just like in English, certain syllables are stressed more than others. If a word ends in a vowel, **n**, or **s**, and there is no written accent, the next-to-last syllable is stressed.

sala

suben

cortinas

apartamento

If a word ends in a consonant other than **n** or **s**, the natural stress falls on the last syllable of the word.

mujer

reloj

bajar

ideal

televisor

Words that have written accents are stressed on the syllable with the accent.

jardín

sillón

lámpara

sofá

décimo

Audio Scripts

TELEHISTORIA COMPLETA

Level 1 Textbook p. 261

Level 1B Textbook p. 58

TXT CD 5, Track 7

Escena 1 – Resumen

Fernando va a la casa de Manuel porque necesitan estudiar. Pero a Manuel le gusta más jugar videojuegos.

Escena 2 – Resumen

Manuel no puede encontrar su cuaderno. Fernando piensa que Manuel es muy desorganizado.

Escena 3 – Resumen

Manuel: ¡Mamá! ¡La camiseta! ¿Dónde está?

Sra. Cuevas: ¿Qué camiseta?

Manuel: La camiseta de Alicia, mi amiga de Miami.

Sra. Cuevas: Ay, hijo. Aquí en el jardín no está. Tiene que estar en la casa.

Manuel: ¡Mamá! ¡Por favor!

Sra. Cuevas: Manuel, estoy ocupada.

Manuel: ¿Dónde está? Aquí en la mesa no está.

Fernando: No está encima de la mesa. No está en tu cuarto.

Manuel: ¡No, tiene que estar aquí!

Fernando: ¿En el comedor? ¿En la cocina? Manuel, aquí hay un gato al lado del sillón.

Manuel: Sí, es Fígaro, el gato de Elena. ¿Y qué?

Fernando: El gato está encima de ¡una camiseta!

ACTIVIDAD 20 (24) – INTEGRACIÓN

Level 1 Textbook p. 263

TXT CD 5, Track 8

Level 1B Textbook p. 60

Level 1B TXT CD, Track 8

Tú y tu familia van a vivir un año en Quito y necesitan un apartamento. Mira la lista de una agencia de alquiler y escucha el mensaje telefónico de un agente. Describe cuál es el mejor apartamento para ustedes.

FUENTE 2

TXT CD 5, Track 9

Level 1B TXT CD, Track 9

Listen and take notes

¿Cómo es el apartamento y dónde está?

¿Cuánto cuesta?

¡Hola! Soy el señor Chávez. Si usted y su familia quieren alquilar un apartamento en el centro de Quito, tengo un apartamento muy bonito. Está en la calle Venezuela. No es muy grande, pero no es tan pequeño como mi apartamento. Tiene cuatro cuartos y dos baños. La sala es grande y tiene muchas ventanas. La cocina es un poco pequeña. El apartamento no tiene patio, pero está al lado del parque y cerca del centro comercial. El apartamento está en el quinto piso y pueden ver el parque. Está un poco lejos de la escuela, pero pueden tomar el autobús. ¡Ah!... una cosa más. No cuesta mucho; ustedes pueden alquilarlo por 1.150 dólares al mes. Bueno, hablamos más tarde. Adiós.

LECTURA: VIVIR EN ECUADOR

Level 1 Textbook pp. 264–265

Level 1B Textbook pp. 62–63

TXT CD 5, Track 10

The following are an apartment brochure from Quito and a real-estate ad from Guayaquil.

Las Camelias. Comunidad Residencial.

El Quiteño moderno

Construcción antisísmica; Jardines comunales; Sauna; Gimnasio; Portero de 24 horas; Áreas verdes y recreativas; Cerca de tiendas, supermercados y restaurantes.

¿Quieres estar cerca de todo? El Quiteño Moderno está en un lugar muy conveniente. Desde el noveno piso puedes ver todo el centro. Apartamento de 95 metros cuadrados, $65.000.

Residencias Pichincha

Avenida El Inca, 32

Teléfono: 244-5502

Cerro Santa Ana, Comunidad privada de 18 residencias.

Aquí puedes ir de compras o al cine y en unos minutos volver a tu casa cerca del río Guayas. Cerro Santa Ana es para las personas a quienes les gusta el aire puro tanto como un lugar urbano.

$130.000

Casa ultramoderna de dos pisos con acceso fácil a Guayaquil

4 cuartos; 3 baños; sala-comedor; cocina; oficina; área de máquinas de lavar; 2 garajes

La casa está en un lugar tranquilo pero no está muy lejos de Guayaquil. Puedes preparar la comida en el patio y hay zonas para practicar deportes.

Cerro Santa Ana

Escalón 68

Teléfono: 231-6687

REPASO: ACTIVIDAD 1 — LISTEN AND UNDERSTAND

Level 1 Textbook p. 268

TXT CD 5, Track 11

Level 1B Textbook p. 66

Level 1B TXT CD, Track 10

Escucha a Rebeca describir su casa. Indica si las oraciones con ciertas o falsas.

Vivo en una casa muy bonita. La sala es grande y tiene muchas ventanas. En la sala hay un televisor, un sofá y tres lámparas. El comedor está al lado de la sala. Los muebles del comedor son: una mesa grande y seis sillas. También hay unas cortinas azules. Detrás del comedor está la cocina. Cuando subimos la escalera, encontramos tres cuartos. En los cuartos hay cómodas, armarios y lámparas. Mi cuarto es amarillo. También hay dos baños en el segundo piso. Vamos a bajar la escalera ahora para ir al patio. Tenemos un patio grande y un jardín bonito. Mi casa es la casa ideal, ¿no?

Audio Scripts

WORKBOOK SCRIPTS WB CD 3

INTEGRACIÓN HABLAR

Level 1 Workbook p. 206

Level 1B Workbook p. 10

WB CD 3, Track 1

Listen to the radio ad that Débora listened to before going to the mall. Take notes.

FUENTE 2

WB CD 3, Track 2

¡Hola! El Centro Comercial Altavista es el mejor. Puede comprar camas, sillones, cómodas y muchos muebles más. Puede comprar jeans, camisas, vestidos y toda la ropa que necesita, para hombres, mujeres y niños. También tenemos radios, televisores, tocadiscos compactos, lámparas y lectores de DVD. ¡A todos les gusta nuestro centro comercial!

INTEGRACIÓN ESCRIBIR

Level 1 Workbook p. 207

Level 1B Workbook p. 11

WB CD 3, Track 3

Listen to Manuel, the clerk at the department store, calling to the stockroom on the second floor. Take notes.

FUENTE 2

WB CD 3, Track 4

¡Hola, Antonio! Soy Manuel, en la planta baja. Por favor, baja tres cortinas blancas. Un espejo grande. Dos sillones negros. Una lámpara grande y otra pequeña. Una cama grande y dos camas pequeñas. Una alfombra grande. Una cómoda y un armario. Un televisor y dos videojuegos.

ESCUCHAR A, ACTIVIDAD 1

Level 1 Workbook p. 208

Level 1B Workbook p. 12

WB CD 3, Track 5

Listen to Cristian. Then, look at the list and draw a line through the articles that his parents do not buy.

Buenas tardes. Me llamo Cristian. Mis padres compran muchas cosas para nuestra casa nueva. Es nuestra tercera casa. Primero, compran las cortinas para la ventana de la sala. Son muy bonitas. Después, compran un sillón negro y una alfombra gris. Me gusta el sillón para leer un libro o mirar la televisión. Yo quiero comprar un televisor nuevo pero mi papá no quiere. Mis padres también compran un lector DVD para mi cuarto.

ESCUCHAR A, ACTIVIDAD 2

Level 1 Workbook p. 208

Level 1B Workbook p. 12

WB CD 3, Track 6

Listen to Olga Uribe talk about her home. Then choose the correct answer to each question.

Buenos días. Me llamo Olga Uribe. Mi esposo y yo compramos muchas cosas para la casa nueva. Es la segunda casa que tenemos en cinco años. Pero ésta es la casa más bonita. Nuestros hijos vuelven este año y necesitamos más cuartos para ellos. Ellos son estudiantes y están en otra ciudad. Queremos comprar camas nuevas, cortinas, radios y alfombras para hacer más bonitos sus cuartos.

ESCUCHAR B, ACTIVIDAD 1

Level 1 Workbook p. 209

Level 1B Workbook p. 13

WB CD 3, Track 7

Listen to Carmen and take notes. Then, place an "X" next to the things she has in her room.

Hola, me llamo Carmen. Después de la escuela, estoy todo el día en mi casa. Es la casa ideal, me gusta mucho. En mi cuarto tengo muchos discos compactos.

Además, tengo un lector DVD y veo mis películas preferidas. Mi cama es muy bonita y las cortinas son nuevas. Primero, estudio en la tarde y después, hago todas las cosas que me gustan.

ESCUCHAR B, ACTIVIDAD 2

Level 1 Workbook p. 209

Level 1B Workbook p. 13

WB CD 3, Track 8

Listen to Lorena and Norberto. Then, answer the questions in complete sentences.

Norberto: Hola, Lorena. Habla Norberto. ¿Tienes el primer disco compacto de tu músico preferido?

Lorena: Hola, Norberto. No, tengo el segundo y el tercero pero no tengo el primero.

Norberto: Pues yo lo tengo. ¿Lo quieres?

Lorena: ¡Sí! Por favor.

Norberto: Voy a darte el disco.

Lorena: ¡Gracias! Estoy muy contenta.

Norberto: Yo también estoy contento.

Lorena: Eres un buen amigo.

ESCUCHAR C, ACTIVIDAD 1

Level 1 Workbook p. 210

Level 1B Workbook p. 14

WB CD 3, Track 9

Listen to the conversation between Claudia and Ana. Take notes. Then complete the table below with what each one does.

Ana: Hoy almuerzo con mi hermano Pablo. Él va a comprar un apartamento mañana y quiero comprar un regalo para él. ¿Puedes venir al centro comercial esta tarde?

Claudia: Sí, comprar un regalo es buena idea. Yo también quiero comprar algo para él. Tu hermano es un buen amigo.

Ana: Sí, es cierto. Quiero comprar un espejo o una alfombra.

Claudia: Yo creo que quiero comprar un radio.

Ana: Es una idea interesante. ¿Voy a ir a las tres? Pero, primero voy a almorzar con él.

Claudia: Sí. A las tres está bien.

Audio Scripts

ESCUCHAR C, ACTIVIDAD 2

Level 1 Workbook p. 210

Level 1B Workbook p. 14

WB CD 3, Track 10

Listen to Martín and take notes. Then complete the sentences.

Hoy voy a tener un día muy divertido. Primero, voy a ver un apartamento para comprar. Es el apartamento ideal. Segundo, voy a almorzar con mis amigos. En tercer lugar, voy a ver a mi amigo Juan para ir a comprar unos discos compactos. Por último, tengo que comprar unas cortinas para mi nuevo apartamento.

ASSESSMENT SCRIPTS TEST CD

LESSON 1 TEST: ESCUCHAR ACTIVIDAD A

Modified p. 170

On-level p. 215

Pre-AP p. 170

TEST CD 2, Track 1

Listen to the following audio. Then complete Activity A.

Survey Administrator: Dígame, señor Ortega, ¿viven ustedes en una casa o un apartamento?

Señor Ortega: Vivimos en una casa.

Survey Administrator: ¿Tienen un jardín en su casa?

Señor Ortega: Sí, tenemos un jardín muy bonito.

Survey Administrator: ¿Tienen muebles en el jardín?

Señor Ortega: Sí, hay una mesa y sillas. Nos gusta comer en el jardín.

Survey Administrator: ¿Cuántos pisos tienen en su casa?

Señor Ortega: Tenemos dos pisos. La cocina, la sala y el comedor están en el primer piso y hay tres cuartos y un baño en el segundo piso.

Survey Administrator: ¿Qué muebles tienen en la sala?

Señor Ortega: En la sala tenemos dos sofás, dos sillones, una mesa y dos lámparas.

Survey Administrator: ¿Qué muebles tienen en su cuarto?

Señor Ortega: Tenemos una cama, dos mesas pequeñas, una cómoda, dos lámparas y un escritorio.

Survey Administrator: Muchas gracias por contestar nuestras preguntas, señor.

Señor Ortega: Con mucho gusto. Adiós.

LESSON 1 TEST: ESCUCHAR ACTIVIDAD B

Modified p. 170

On-level p. 215

Pre-AP p. 170

TEST CD 2 Track 2

Listen to the following audio. Then complete Activity B.

Mi familia tiene una casa en Quito. Nuestra casa tiene dos pisos. También hay un jardín al lado de la casa. En el primer piso tenemos una sala, un comedor y la cocina. En el segundo piso, hay dos cuartos: el cuarto de mis padres y el cuarto que comparto con mi hermana menor. En nuestro cuarto, hay dos camas, dos escritorios y una lámpara. Tenemos un armario grande para nuestra ropa. Queremos un televisor en el cuarto, pero no lo tenemos. El televisor está en la sala. Tenemos que bajar la escalera para mirar la televisión.

HERITAGE LEARNERS SCRIPTS HL CDs 2 & 4

INTEGRACIÓN HABLAR

Level 1 Workbook p. 208

Level 1B Workbook p. 12

HL CD 2, Track 1

Escucha el mensaje que le dejó el señor Aguilar a su nieto Mario. Toma notas mientas escuchas y luego responde a las preguntas.

FUENTE 2

HL CD 2, Track 2

Mario, ¿estás ahí? ¿Mario? Hombre, nunca te encuentro. Bien, te llamo sólo para avisarte que tu abuela y yo decidimos jubilarnos. Te mando por Internet el anuncio y la foto de la casa que hallamos en Ecuador. Es difícil decidir entre esa casa o el condominio de Chicago. El condominio de Chicago está en un edificio de quince pisos, tiene una recámara, sala, cocina y baño. El precio es $350 mil dólares. Nos parece un poco caro pero está en el centro de Chicago y así están los precios ahí. Tu abuela y yo estamos listos para tener una vida tranquila. ¿Qué piensas tú? Contamos contigo para que le cuentes la noticia a tu mamá. Ya sabes ella que se preocupa mucho por nosotros.

INTEGRACIÓN ESCRIBIR

Level 1 Workbook p. 209

HL CD 2, Track 3

Escucha el anuncio de radio de una compañía constructora de casas. Puedes tomar notas mientras escuchas y luego completa la actividad.

FUENTE 2

HL CD 2, Track 4

Los residentes de Lago Escondido tienen muchas razones para estar orgullosos. Visítenos hoy y vea por qué. La nueva fase Villas de Lago Escondido pone a su disposición veinte nuevas casas, todas con vista al lago, jardín diseñado y patio. El modelo Villa Rústica le ofrece dos pisos, con garaje en la planta baja, tres dormitorios, cuarto de lavandería, cuarto de televisión y cocina integral. Viva la vida tranquila de Lago Escondido, donde cada vecino está a media cuadra de distancia. Visítenos hoy y participe en la rifa de un televisor de alta definición. Villas de Lago Escondido, la casa de sus sueños. En la salida 23 de la carretera sur.

Audio Scripts

LESSON 1 TEST: ESCUCHAR ACTIVIDAD A

HL Assessment Book p. 176

HL CD 4, Track 1

Escucha el siguiente audio. Luego, completa la Actividad A.

El Sr. Arias: Buenos días, Mueblería Fernández.

La Sra. Muñoz: Buenos días. Soy la señora Muñoz. ¿Me puede decir cuándo van a llegar los muebles?

El Sr. Arias: ¿Y qué muebles son, señora?

La Sra. Muñoz: Son los muebles para nuestra casa: un sofá, dos sillones, dos lámparas, una alfombra.

El Sr. Arias: ¡Ay! Son muebles para su sala.

La Sra. Muñoz: Sí, y también muebles para la casa de mi hijo: el cuarto, el comedor, la cocina y el patio. ¿Dónde están la cama, la mesa del comedor, las cortinas de la cocina y los sillones para el patio?

El Sr. Arias: Vamos a ver... Aquí están. El sofá, los sillones, las lámparas y la alfombra van a la calle Alta Vista, número 5.

La Sra. Muñoz: No, no. Nuestra dirección es calle Quinta Vista, sin número.

El Sr. Arias: ¿Y cuál es la dirección de su hijo?

La Sra. Muñoz: Es la calle Almendros 4, décimo piso.

El Sr. Arias: ¡Ay! Aquí tengo Almendros 10, cuarto piso.

La Sra. Muñoz: Por favor, tiene que escribir las direcciones correctamente.

El Sr. Arias: Sí, sí, señora. Perdón, y no se preocupe. Ahora escribo todo bien y los muebles van a llegar a su casa y al apartamento de su hijo bien.

La Sra. Muñoz: ¿Llegan mañana?

El Sr. Arias: No, señora. Con un poco de suerte, van a llegar hoy.

La Sra. Muñoz: Muy bien. Gracias.

El Sr. Arias: A usted, señora Muñoz.

ESCUCHAR ACTIVIDAD B

HL Assessment Book p. 176

HL CD 4, Track 2

Escucha el siguiente audio. Luego, completa la Actividad B.

Mi familia vive en un apartamento en el centro de la ciudad. Nuestro apartamento es bastante grande y está en el décimo piso, que es el último. En la planta baja de nuestro edificio hay una tienda de muebles y un café. No tenemos jardín pero si bajamos a la calle hay un jardín muy grande delante de nuestro edificio de apartamentos. Somos tres hermanos y cada uno tiene su cuarto. Tengo una cama, dos cómodas y un armario enorme (porque me gusta la ropa y tengo muchísima). También hay un escritorio donde estudio todos los días y una alfombra preciosa azul y blanca. A cada lado de mi cama hay una mesita de noche donde pongo el radio, el tocadiscos compactos y mi colección de discos compactos. También tengo tres lámparas; una está encima del escritorio y las otras dos están en las mesitas de noche. Y encima de las ventanas hay unas cortinas también azules y blancas. Estoy muy contenta con mi cuarto.

Audio Scripts

UNIDAD 5, LECCIÓN 2
TEXTBOOK SCRIPTS
TXT CD 5

PRESENTACIÓN DE VOCABULARIO

Level 1 Textbook pp. 272–273

Level 1B Textbook pp. 70–72

TXT CD 5, Track 12

A. ¡Hola! Soy Elena. Vamos a dar una fiesta porque es el cumpleaños de Manuel, pero es un secreto. Antes de celebrar, hay que limpiar la cocina porque está sucia.

B. Acabamos de limpiar la cocina pero todavía tenemos que trabajar. Toda la casa debe estar limpia.

C. Mi papá quiere ayudar con los quehaceres pero no cocina muy bien. Prefiere poner la mesa.

D. Son las cuatro y los invitados van a venir a las cinco. Papá pone las decoraciones y Fernando envuelve un regalo para Manuel.

E. Cuando Manuel llega, todos dicen «¡Sorpresa!» Yo canto «Feliz cumpleaños» y mis padres bailan.

¡A RESPONDER!

Level 1 Textbook p. 273

Level 1B Textbook p. 72

Level 1B TXT CD Track 11

TXT CD 5, Track 13

Escucha la lista de actividades. Mientras escuchas, representa las actividades.

1. planchar la ropa
2. bailar
3. barrer el suelo
4. poner la mesa
5. envolver el regalo
6. cocinar
7. lavar los platos
8. pasar la aspiradora

TELEHISTORIA ESCENA 1

Level 1 Textbook p. 275

Level 1B Textbook p. 74

TXT CD 5, Track 14

Fernando: ¿Y los regalos? ¿Dónde...?

Sra. Cuevas: En la mesa.

Elena: Fernando, ¿qué regalo traes para Manuel?

Fernando: Un videojuego. Lo acabo de envolver.

Sr. Cuevas: Un videojuego. ¡Qué sorpresa!

Fernando: ¿Puedo ayudar?

Elena: Sí, puedes abrir la puerta a los invitados.

Fernando: Ay, prefiero preparar la comida. ¡Me gusta cocinar!

Sr. Cuevas: Bueno. Puedes ayudar en la cocina.

Sra. Cuevas: ¿Qué hora es? ¿Dónde está tu hermano?

Fernando: Acabo de hablar por teléfono con Manuel. Va a venir.

TELEHISTORIA ESCENA 2

Level 1 Textbook p. 280

Level 1B Textbook p. 80

TXT CD 5, Track 15

Manuel: ¡El autógrafo de Trini Salgado!

Elena: ¡Allí viene Manuel!

Todos: ¡Sorpresa!

Sra. Cuevas: ¡Feliz cumpleaños, hijo!

Elena: ¡Aquí viene el pastel!

Manuel: Y, ¿qué hago ahora?

Fernando: ¡Abrir los regalos! Yo los traigo.

Manuel: ¡Qué sorpresa! ¡Un videojuego! No lo tengo. Muchas gracias, Fernando.

Fernando: Hmmm… Y, ¿qué hacemos ahora?

Sr. Cuevas: ¡A bailar todos!

PRONUNCIACIÓN

Las letras b y v

Level 1 Textbook p. 283

Level 1B Textbook p. 79

TXT CD 5, Track 16

Las letras **b** o b grande y **v**, uve o v chica

In Spanish, the **b** and **v** are pronounced almost the same. As the first letter of a word, at the beginning of a sentence or after the letters **m** and **n**, **b** and **v** are pronounced like the hard **b** in the English word *boy*.

In the middle of a word, **b** and **v** have a softer sound, made by keeping the lips slightly apart.

Listen and repeat.

basura
venir
alfombra
invitar
deber
todavía
globo
acabar
Bárbara baila la cumbia en Colombia.
Debes subir al octavo piso.

ACTIVIDAD 14 (15) - UNA CASA SUCIA

Level 1 Textbook p. 284

TXT CD 5, Track 17

Level 1B Textbook p. 83

Level 1B TXT CD, Track 12

La casa de Elena está sucia y su madre necesita ayuda. Escucha las situaciones y escribe un mandato para cada una.

1. Elena, la alfombra está muy sucia. Todavía necesitas pasar la aspiradora.
2. Ay, ¿qué pasa en la cocina? Todavía necesitas barrer el suelo.
3. Todavía hay que sacar la basura en la cocina.
4. Hay que lavar los platos. Están muy sucios. ¿Me ayudas, mi hija?
5. Tus abuelos vienen hoy. Necesitas hacer la cama.
6. Vamos a comer temprano. Todavía hay que poner la mesa.

TELEHISTORIA COMPLETA

Level 1 Textbook p. 285

Level 1B Textbook p. 86

TXT CD 5, Track 18

Escena 1 – Resumen

Fernando trae un regalo a la fiesta de sorpresa para Manuel y quiere ayudar a la familia. Manuel todavía no está en casa.

Escena 2 – Resumen

Manuel llega a la fiesta con el autógrafo de Trini Salgado. Hay pastel, y él abre los regalos de los invitados.

Escena 3 – Resumen

Sra. Cuevas: Pon los platos sucios allí.

Sr. Cuevas: Elena, barre el suelo, saca la basura y yo lavo la ropa.

Elena: ¿Y Manuel? ¿Por qué no ayuda?

Sra. Cuevas: Acaba de celebrar su cumpleaños. Hoy no tiene que limpiar.

Elena: ¿Vienes a ayudar? Toma.

Manuel: ¡Elena! Ahora, ¡no! Tengo que buscar la camiseta de Alicia. ¿Dónde está? ¿Mamá…?

Elena: La camiseta de Alicia... ¿Dónde está?

Sr. Cuevas: ¡Ahh! ¡Acabo de lavarla!

ACTIVIDAD 19 (22) — INTEGRACIÓN

Level 1 Textbook p. 287

TXT CD 5, Track 19

Level 1B Textbook p. 88

Level 1B TXT CD, Track 13

Tú y tu amigo o amiga son participantes en un programa de televisión, **¡Limpia ya!** Escucha el mensaje para aprender cuál es tu misión y mira los planos de la casa. Luego, explica lo que tú haces y dile a tu amigo o amiga qué hacer.

FUENTE 2: INSTRUCCIONES PARA LA MISIÓN

TXT CD 5, Track 20

Level 1B TXT CD, Track 14

Listen and take notes.

¿Qué quehaceres tienen que hacer?

¿Dónde tienen que hacerlos?

Hola y bienvenidos al programa. Si limpian la casa en dos horas reciben dos coches nuevos y cinco mil dólares. Pero no es fácil. Hay que ser organizados. Tienen que limpiar todos los cuartos y baños. Deben hacer las camas; hay siete camas. También necesitan limpiar la cocina. En la cocina hay que sacar la basura, lavar los platos y barrer el suelo. En la sala hay una alfombra sucia y encima del sofá está toda la ropa sucia de la familia. Deben pasar la aspiradora, lavar y planchar la ropa. Hay que poner la mesa del comedor. En el jardín, necesitan cortar el césped. Buena suerte y... ¡Limpia ya!

LECTURA CULTURAL: BAILES FOLKLÓRICOS DE ECUADOR Y PANAMÁ

Level 1 Textbook pp. 288–289

Level 1B Textbook pp. 90–91

TXT CD 5, Track 21

Los bailes folklóricos de Latinoamérica representan una combinación de culturas. Ayudan a formar una identidad nacional y continuar las tradiciones de las personas que viven allí. A muchas personas de Ecuador y Panamá les gusta bailar cuando celebran fiestas.

Hay muchos bailes de influencia indígena en Ecuador. Uno de los bailes más populares se llama el sanjuanito. El sanjuanito tiene un ritmo alegre y es una buena representación de la fusión de culturas indígenas y españolas.

Para bailar, chicos y chicas forman un círculo y muchas veces bailan con pañuelos en las manos. Es posible ver el baile del sanjuanito todo el año en celebraciones en casa, pero es más común durante el festival de San Juan en junio.

En Panamá, es muy popular bailar salsa en fiestas o discotecas, pero el baile nacional es el tamborito. El tamborito usa ritmos de influencia africana, pero también tiene orígenes indígenas y españoles.

Las personas bailan con el sonido de palmadas y tambores africanos. El tamborito es popular durante fiestas grandes y celebraciones regionales, como Carnaval. Para bailar en los festivales, las chicas llevan polleras (los vestidos tradicionales de Panamá) y los chicos llevan el dominguero (pantalones negros con una camisa blanca).

REPASO: ACTIVIDAD 1 – LISTEN AND UNDERSTAND

Level 1 Textbook p. 292

TXT CD 5, Track 22

Level 1B Textbook p. 94

Level 1B TXT CD, Track 15

El señor Robles y sus estudiantes hablan de una fiesta. Escucha la conversación y empareja las personas con las oraciones correspondientes.

Sr. Robles: Chicos, la fiesta para la directora es una sorpresa. Todos ustedes van a ayudar, ¿no?

Jóvenes: Sí. Yo, sí. Sí, señor.

Sr. Robles: Andrés, trae los globos, por favor.

Andrés: Sí, señor. Los traigo mañana.

Sr. Robles: Samuel, ayuda a limpiar el cuarto.

Samuel: Está bien. Mañana vengo temprano.

Sr. Robles: Carla, ven temprano también y pon las decoraciones.

Carla: Sí, señor Robles. Me gusta decorar.

Sr. Robles: Y yo traigo pizza para todos.

Jóvenes: ¡Qué bien! ¡Buena idea!

COMPARACIÓN CULTURAL: ¡ASÍ CELEBRAMOS!

Level 1 Textbook pp. 294–295

Level 1B Textbook pp. 96–97

TXT CD 5, Track 23

Narrador: Panamá. María Elena.

María Elena: ¡Saludos desde Panamá! Me llamo María Elena. Mi familia y yo acabamos de decorar la casa para celebrar la Navidad. El 24 de diciembre es muy importante en Panamá. Las familias comen la cena tarde y a las doce de la noche abren los regalos. Mis hermanos y yo siempre decoramos el árbol de Navidad. También me gusta envolver regalos con papel. Quiero dar y recibir muchos regalos este año.

Narrador: Argentina. Carla.

Carla: ¡Hola! Me llamo Carla y vivo en el norte de Argentina. Todos los años celebramos un gran festival. En el festival podemos ver a los gauchos con sus caballos, escuchar música típica y comer comida rica. Siempre llevo un vestido bonito para participar en los bailes típicos con otros chicos y chicas.

Narrador: Ecuador. Daniel.

Daniel: ¡Hola! Me llamo Daniel y vivo en Cuenca, Ecuador. Para la fiesta del año nuevo, muchas personas hacen figuras grandes de papel maché. Las figuras son de muchos colores y muchas veces son muy cómicas. La noche del 31 de diciembre mis padres dan una fiesta. Invitan a muchas personas. Limpiamos toda la casa, ponemos la mesa y compartimos una cena rica con nuestra familia y los otros invitados.

REPASO: ACTIVIDAD 1 – LISTEN, UNDERSTAND, AND COMPARE

Level 1 Textbook p. 296

Level 1B Textbook p. 98

TXT CD 5, Track 24

Audio Scripts

Gabriela is giving a surprise party. Listen to her phone message. Then answer the following questions.

¿Dónde estás? Son las cinco y media y acabo de volver a mi casa. La fiesta de sorpresa para Elisa es a las seis y media. Hay mucho que hacer. Tú vas a ayudarme, ¿verdad? Tengo que ir a la tienda para comprar comida. Sirvo pollo con patatas y una ensalada. Por favor, trae los tomates de tu jardín. Si llegas antes de las seis y media, ve al apartamento de la señora Domínguez, en el cuarto piso. Ella tiene el pastel de cumpleaños. Después baja al segundo piso y habla con Jorge y Marlene. Ellos tienen los discos compactos que necesito para la fiesta. Si los invitados llegan temprano y no estoy, sirve los refrescos. Gracias. Hasta luego.

WORKBOOK SCRIPTS WB CD 3

INTEGRACIÓN HABLAR

Level 1 Workbook p. 229

Level 1B Workbook p. 33

WB CD 3, Track 11

Listen to the message left by Rebecca on Cristina's voicemail. Take notes.

FUENTE 2

WB CD 3, Track 12

¡Hola Cristina! Acabo de decorar todo el patio con globos. Papá acaba de cortar el césped. La sala está limpia, mamá acaba de pasar la aspiradora. Todos los refrescos están en la cocina y los sándwiches están preparados. Pero necesito ayuda. Si tú o un invitado llegan temprano. Tenemos que llevar la mesa de la sala al patio porque, ¡qué divertido, vamos a bailar!

INTEGRACIÓN ESCRIBIR

Level 1 Workbook p. 230

Level 1B Workbook p. 34

WB CD 3, Track 13

Listen to a review in the radio program about the movie. Take notes.

FUENTE 2

WB CD 3, Track 14

La película es muy buena porque tiene una sorpresa. La chica siempre está ocupada con los quehaceres de la casa. Pero meses después, está cansada y no puede hacer más. Necesita ayuda y, ¡sorpresa! Ella encuentra un cuarto secreto. Dentro del cuarto hay dinero, ¡mucho dinero!

ESCUCHAR A, ACTIVIDAD 1

Level 1 Workbook p. 231

Level 1B Workbook p. 35

WB CD 3, Track 15

Listen to Jimena and Mabel. Then read each statement and answer cierto (true) or falso (false).

Mabel: Jimena, ya es tarde. Ya llegan los invitados. ¿Preparas la comida?

Jimena: No, Mabel. Acabo de prepararla toda. Ya está. Y tú, ¿todavía limpias la sala?

Mabel: Sí, ayúdame con esto. No puedo pasar la aspiradora y barrer también.

Jimena: Sí. ¿Quién pone la mesa?

Mabel: Eduardo dice que él la pone. Pregúntale.

Jimena: Eduardo está arriba, en su cuarto. Escucho música en su cuarto... ¿Eduardo? Ven, por favor. Pon la mesa porque es tarde.

ESCUCHAR A, ACTIVIDAD 2

Level 1 Workbook p. 231

Level 1B Workbook p. 35

WB CD 3, Track 16

Listen to Norma. Then answer the following questions in complete sentences.

Hola, me llamo Norma. Hoy es mi cumpleaños. ¿Qué pasa en mi casa? Primero, mis hermanos dicen "hay que limpiar todo" y después me dicen: "Sal de la casa. Ve a buscar unos refrescos". Mis amigos traen cosas y yo no puedo ver qué son. Pienso que es una fiesta sorpresa.

ESCUCHAR B, ACTIVIDAD 1

Level 1 Workbook p. 232

Level 1B Workbook p. 36

WB CD 3, Track 17

Listen to Mariana and take notes. Then, draw a line from the actions in the right column to the person who does it on the left. One person can do more than one thing.

Me llamo Mariana y tengo mucho trabajo esta semana. Por eso prefiero no hacer los quehaceres de la casa. Mis hijos me ayudan mucho. Luis limpia su cuarto todos los días y Cecilia limpia la sala, prepara la comida en la cocina y lava los platos. En la noche, Luis saca la basura. El fin de semana corta el césped. Cuando llego, le doy de comer al perro y plancho la ropa.

ESCUCHAR B, ACTIVIDAD 2

Level 1 Workbook p. 232

Level 1B Workbook p. 36

WB CD 3, Track 18

Listen to Luis and Cecilia. Then answer the following questions in complete sentences.

Cecilia: Luis, trae la aspiradora por favor; está en la planta alta. Hay que ayudar porque Mamá dice que la alfombra de la sala está muy sucia.

Luis: Búscala tú, Cecilia. Yo no puedo. Tengo que hacer mi tarea.

Cecilia: Tráela, por favor. No quiero subir la escalera.

Luis: Te digo que no puedo. Hago mi cama y barro mi cuarto.

Cecilia: Está bien. Más tarde tú también vas a pedir un favor.

Luis: Está bien. La traigo, pero tú ¡ayuda con mi cuarto!

ESCUCHAR C, ACTIVIDAD 1

Level 1 Workbook p. 233

Level 1B Workbook p. 37

WB CD 3, Track 19

Listen to Teresa and her father and take notes. Then, complete the following sentences.

Papá: Teresa, ayuda a tu mamá.

Teresa: Sí, papá. Acabo de lavar los platos y de sacar la basura. ¿ Tú cortas el césped?

Papá: Acabo de cortarlo. Tu mamá está muy cansada.

Teresa: Entonces Mamá puede dormir unos minutos en la cama.

Papá: Bueno, vamos a cenar en una hora. ¿Dónde está tu hermano?

Teresa: Está en su cuarto; escucha su disco compacto preferido.

Papá: Él debe ayudar a poner la mesa.

Audio Scripts

ESCUCHAR C, ACTIVIDAD 2

Level 1 Workbook p. 233

Level 1B Workbook p. 37

WB CD 3, Track 20

Listen to Osvaldo and take notes. Then, in complete sentences, describe what he says about the the following things.

Me llamo Osvaldo y mi hermana y mi papá hacen muchos quehaceres en la casa. A mí no me gusta hacerlos. Yo pongo mis discos compactos y escucho música. Creo que las tareas de la casa son para las chicas. Mis amigos sí ayudan es sus casas: lavan los platos, ponen la mesa, sacan la basura, limpian sus cuartos y hacen sus camas. Cuando traigo a amigos a casa, ellos dicen que yo tengo que ayudar. Tal vez mañana.

ASSESSMENT SCRIPTS
TEST CD 2

LESSON 2 TEST: ESCUCHAR
ACTIVIDAD A

Modified Assessment Book p. 182

On-level Assessment Book p. 232

Pre-AP Assessment Book p. 182

TEST CD 2, Track 3

Listen to the following audio. Then complete Activity A.

Mañana es la fiesta de sorpresa para mamá. Hay que trabajar mucho para preparar la fiesta. Papá, por favor ve a la tienda y compra un pastel. En el pastel escribe "Feliz cumpleaños". Tía Cristina, la cocina está muy sucia. Por favor, limpia la cocina. Hay que barrer el piso y lavar los platos. Tío Tomás, por favor prepara la sala. Pon las decoraciones y trae muchas sillas del comedor. Abuelo, por favor, envuelve los regalos. Abuela, siempre cocinas platos muy ricos. Por favor, cocina arroz con pollo para la fiesta. Es el plato favorito de mi mamá.

Padre: Julia, vamos a trabajar mucho. Y tú ¿qué vas a hacer?

Julia: Papá, estoy muy cansada. Necesito descansar.

ACTIVIDAD B

Modified Assessment Book p. 182

On-level Assessment Book p. 232

Pre-AP Assessment Book p. 182

TEST CD 2, Track 4

Listen to the following audio. Then complete Activity B.

David: Hola, Patricia. No puedo ir a tu fiesta el sábado. Estoy mal.

Patricia: Ay, David. Va a ser una fiesta muy divertida.

David: ¿Invitas a muchos amigos?

Patricia: Sí, David. Invito a treinta amigos. Tenemos que hacer muchos quehaceres antes de la fiesta. Vamos a limpiar la casa y mi mamá va a preparar un pastel.

David: ¿Van a bailar mucho?

Patricia: Sí, vamos a bailar toda la noche. David, necesitas dormir mucho.

David: Sí, voy a descansar en mi casa. Estoy un poco triste porque no puedo ir a la fiesta. ¡Feliz cumpleaños!

UNIDAD 5 TEST: ESCUCHAR
ACTIVIDAD A

Modified Assessment Book p. 194

On-level Assessment Book p. 244

Pre-AP Assessment Book p. 194

TEST CD 2, Track 5

Listen to the following audio. Then complete Activity A.

Padre: Hola, María. ¿Quieres ayudar?

María: Sí, papá.

Padre: Por favor, barre el suelo, lava los platos y saca la basura.

Padre: Hola, Roberto. Mamá dice que tienes que limpiar tu cuarto. Por favor, haz la cama y pasa la aspiradora.

Roberto: ¡Pero, Papá! Mi cuarto no está sucio.

Padre: Por favor, Roberto, escucha a tu mamá.

Padre: Hola, Tomás. Por favor, ve al jardín y corta el césped.

Tomás: Papá, acabo de barrer el suelo. ¡Son muchos quehaceres!

Padre: Gracias por ayudar, Tomás.

Padre: Paula, vamos a comer la cena a las ocho. Por favor, pon la mesa.

Paula: Sí papá. ¿Cuántas personas van a comer?

Padre: Diez personas. Debes traer más sillas.

Padre: Fernando, todos tus videojuegos están en el sofá. Ponlos en la mesa. La alfombra también está sucia. Debes pasar la aspiradora.

ACTIVIDAD B

Modified Assessment Book p. 194

On-level Assessment Book p. 244

Pre-AP Assessment Book p. 194

TEST CD 2, Track 6

Listen to the following audio. Then complete Activity B.

En la calle Principal vendemos un apartamento muy bonito. El apartamento está en el tercer piso y es ideal para una familia grande. La cocina y el comedor son grandes. El comedor ya tiene una mesa muy grande con ocho sillas. La sala es bonita y puedes ver todo el centro. Hay cinco cuartos y todos los cuartos tienen armarios. El apartamento tiene seis baños. Si quieres ver el apartamento hoy, ¡debes llamar ahora!

HERITAGE LEARNERS SCRIPTS
HL CDs 2 & 4

INTEGRACIÓN HABLAR

Level 1 HL Workbook p. 231

Level 1B HL Workbook p. 35

HL CD 2, Track 5

Escucha el mensaje que le dejó Ana Marta a Teresa. Toma apuntes y realiza la actividad.

FUENTE 2

HL CD 2, Track 6

Teresa, te habla Ana Marta. Mira que estoy con un problema enorme. Como sabes, el mes próximo Martita cumple quince años y a último momento decidió pedirme una fiesta. No sé qué voy a hacer, estoy desesperada. Ya llamé a varios salones y todo está reservado. ¡Aconséjame, mujer! ¿Qué hago? Háblame en cuanto puedas. ¡Chao!

INTEGRACIÓN ESCRIBIR

Level 1 HL Workbook p. 232

Level 1B HL Workbook p. 36

HL CD 2, Track 7

Escucha el mensaje que le deja Ana a su mamá. Toma notas y después completa la actividad.

Audio Scripts

FUENTE 2

HL CD 2, Track 8

Hola mamá: Muchas gracias por querer celebrar mi cumpleaños con una fiesta de quinceañera. Yo sé que tú y papá quieren conservar las tradiciones, pero tú también sabes que yo soy una chica moderna. Todos mis amigos se reirían de mí. Ellos creen que esas fiestas con damas, vals, invitados y pastel son fiestas ridículas. Mejor regálenme un carro. Tú sabes que pronto voy a ir a la universidad y tendré que hacer muchas cosas por mí misma. Ya no quiero tomar más el autobús. No te enojes conmigo, mami. ¡Los quiero mucho!

LESSON 2 TEST: ESCUCHAR ACTIVIDAD A

HL Assessment Book p. 188

HL CD 4, Track 3

Escucha el siguiente audio. Luego, completa la Actividad A.

José: ¡Isabel! Hay que hacer muchas cosas para limpiar la casa.

Isabel: ¿Qué hacemos primero?

José: Haz las camas y pasa la aspiradora. Luego, saca la basura y barre el suelo de la cocina porque está muy sucio. También debes lavar los platos y luego pon la mesa porque vamos a cenar temprano. Yo voy a darle de comer al perro porque tiene mucha hambre.

Isabel: ¿Y qué más vas a hacer tú?

José: Pues... Voy a salir con el perro también. Necesita pasear por lo menos dos horas todos los días.

Isabel: Pero si sales ahora y vuelves en dos horas, estás en casa a las cuatro, y es cuando vienen papá y mamá.

José: Sí, y te ayudo a preparar la cena.

Isabel: ¿Y cómo me vas a ayudar?

José: Traigo el postre—el mejor pastel de la pastelería.

Isabel: ¡No me digas! ¿Y me ayudas a cocinar también?

José: Oye, Isabel, tú eres una cocinera excelente. ¿Cómo te puedo ayudar? ¡Eres la mejor!

Isabel: ¡Qué me dices!

José: Ay, pues te digo una cosa más: plánchame la camisa blanca, por favor, porque quiero llevarla esta noche.

Isabel: ¡Eres imposible, José!

ESCUCHAR ACTIVIDAD B

HL Assessment Book p. 188

HL CD 4, Track 4

Escucha el siguiente audio. Luego, completa la Actividad B.

Tengo mucho que hacer antes de la fiesta. Vamos a ver... ya tengo los regalos, pero necesito más papel de regalo para envolverlos. Debo llamar a Marta y Eugenia porque no sé si van a venir a la fiesta. Luego tengo que buscar un pastel. Debe ser un pastel enorme porque van a venir unas treinta personas. ¡Ay! También debo comprar regalitos para cada uno de los invitados... van a ser muchos. Quiero comprar globos porque pienso decorar el comedor y el jardín con globos rojos. Es el color favorito de José Luis. Luego vengo a casa y la limpio muy bien. Barro el suelo de la cocina, lavo los platos sucios, paso la aspiradora por todos los cuartos y saco la basura. Luego tengo que cocinar... ¡para treinta! A ver si descanso un poco después porque quiero bailar mucho durante la fiesta... ¡Ay! Tengo que buscar los discos compactos. ¿Cómo voy a hacer todos estos quehaceres?

UNIT 5 TEST: ESCUCHAR ACTIVIDAD A

HL Assessment Book p. 200

HL CD 4 Track 5

Escucha el siguiente audio. Luego, completa la Actividad A.

Carlos: ¿A qué piso vamos con el sofá rojo?

Guillermo: Vamos al séptimo. Y tenemos que ir a pie.

Carlos: ¿Y los dos sillones negros?

Guillermo: Al séptimo también.

Carlos: ¿Y para quién es la mesa grande con las doce sillas?

Guillermo: Es para la señora Vázquez y ella vive en el sexto piso.

Carlos: ¿Y los dos armarios tan grandes?

Guillermo: Son para ella también. ¡Tenemos que subir al sexto piso!

Carlos: ¿Es la cómoda para la señora Vázquez también?

Guillermo: No, es para el señor Ríos.

Carlos: ¿En qué piso está?

Guillermo: En el séptimo.

Carlos: ¿Y de quién es el sofá azul? ¡Es enorme! ¿Es del señor Ríos también?

Guillermo: No, es del señor Gómez, pero él vive en el séptimo piso y el televisor es para él también.

Carlos: ¡Pero es que todos los muebles van al sexto o séptimo piso!

Guillermo: No todos porque aquí hay muebles y otros artículos para los apartamentos en el segundo piso y el primer piso.

Carlos: ¿Y qué son?

Guillermo: Mira: dos lámparas para el apartamento 2-C, una alfombra pequeña para el 1-D, un espejo para el 2-B y unas cortinas para el 1-A. ¡Ah! Y un radio para el 2-A.

Carlos: ¿Qué subimos primero?

Guillermo: Sube primero los artículos pequeños. Voy a buscar ayuda. Los dos no podemos con todos los muebles.

Carlos: ¡Buena idea!

ESCUCHAR ACTIVIDAD B

HL Assessment Book p. 200

HL CD 4, Track 6

Escucha el siguiente audio. Luego, completa la Actividad B.

¿Por qué tengo que hacer todo en la casa? Mis hermanos sólo hacen sus camas. Nada más. ¡No es justo! Si mamá le dice a Miguel "Lava los platos" a veces él dice: "Ay, mamá, lo siento pero no tengo tiempo. Tengo que practicar el fútbol". Si papá le dice "Corta el césped" él dice: "Lo siento, pero no puedo. Tengo que trabajar en la biblioteca hoy". Luego si mis padres le dicen a Alberto: "Pasa la aspiradora, Alberto, porque las alfombras están muy sucias", Alberto les dice: "Lo siento, pero hoy tengo que ir a mi clase de guitarra". Y si le dicen "Saca la basura, por favor" Alberto les dice o que está muy cansado o que no se encuentra bien y va a dormir. Luego, ¿quién hace todos estos quehaceres? ¡Yo! Tengo que lavar los platos, pasar la aspiradora, cortar el césped, sacar la basura y, muchas veces, barrer el suelo de la cocina. Mis hermanos no quieren hacer nada. Bueno, hay algo que les gusta hacer: sentarse en el sofá, comer papas fritas, beber refrescos y mirar el fútbol en la televisión. ¿Qué voy a hacer con ellos?

Nombre ______________________ Clase ______________ Fecha ______________

Map/Culture Activities *Ecuador*

❶ About half of Ecuador's population lives in the plateaus and valleys of the Andes Mountains, which divide Ecuador. The other half lives west of these mountains in the coastal lowlands. Which ocean reaches this coastline? Locate it and write its name on the map.

❷ In addition to the mainland territory, a group of islands forms part of the country of Ecuador. Locate these islands and write their name on the map.

❸ Ecuador's capital is located in the northern highlands of the country. Locate this city and write its name in red on the map. The largest city in Ecuador is found in the coastal lowlands of the southwestern part of the country. Find this city and write its name in blue on the map.

Nombre ______________________ Clase ______________ Fecha ______________

Map/Culture Activities *Ecuador*

❹ Are the sentences below true or false? Use the information from the cultural pages in your book to decide. Circle C for **cierto** and F for **falso**. If a sentence is false, circle the word or phrase that is incorrect and write the correct word or phrase below.

1. Cuando vas de compras en Quito, tienes que pagar con dólares. C F

____

2. El campeonato (*championship*) de fútbol es la Serie Mundial. C F

____

3. Ecuador está entre (*between*) Colombia y Bolivia. C F

____

4. La bandera (*flag*) de Ecuador es amarillo, rojo y verde. C F

____

5. Alexandra Ayala Marín y de Gilda Holst son escritoras. C F

____

❺ A variety of typical Ecuadorian dishes is listed and pictured on page 244 of your book, including **locro**, **llapingachos**, **canguil** and **tostado**. The two main ingredients used to make these dishes are potatoes and corn. Why do you think these two ingredients are so commonly used?

____

____

____

____

❻ On page 245 of your book there is a painting of women on their way to an outdoor market in the town of Otavalo. Outdoor markets with flowers, food, clothing, and more can be found throughout Ecuador. Are there any similar markets where you live? What can people buy there?

____

____

____

Map/Culture Activities Answer Key

ECUADOR

Page 83

1. Refer to map above.
2. Refer to map above.
3. Refer to map above.

Page 84

4.
   1. CIRCLE *C*
   2. CIRCLE *F* and **LA SERIE MUNDIAL; la Copa Mundial**
   3. CIRCLE *F* and **BOLIVIA; Perú**
   4. CIRCLE *F* and **VERDE; azul**
   5. CIRCLE *C*
5. Answers will vary, but students should be able to state that potatoes and corn are the two main ingredients, and infer that these are some of the most common crops grown in Ecuador.
6. Answers will vary.

Fine Art Activities

Canoas y casas en el suburbio, Oswaldo Guayasamín

Oswaldo Guayasamín was born in Ecuador in 1919 and began painting at the age of seven. As an Ecuadoran of indigenous heritage, Guayasamín used art to explore his own ethnic identity. His paintings often portray the cultural, social, and political forces that define Latin America. *Canoas y casas en el suburbio* depicts a typical Ecuadoran coastal village.

Answer the following questions based on the painting *Canoas y casas en el suburbio*, by Oswaldo Guayasamín.

1. Examine the entire scope of *Canoas y casas en el suburbio*. Observe the ways in which shape and line interact in the painting. Do the angular shapes work with the smooth lines or against them? How? Explain your response in several complete sentences.

____

____

____

____

____

2. a. Make a list on the lines below of five things you would expect to see in a typical neighborhood that are not included in this painting.

____

____

b. Why do you think Guayasamín chose to exclude certain details or images from his painting and focus on others? How does it make you feel about this **suburbio**?

____

____

____

Canoas y casas en el suburbio (Canoes and Houses in the Suburbs) (1989), Oswaldo Guayasamín. Oil on canvas, 150 cm x 100 cm. Guayaquil de mis amores Collection, Brussels, Belgium. Courtesy of Fundación Guayasamín, Quito, Ecuador.

Fine Art Activities

Indian Dancers and Musicians, Quechua Village, Hugo Licta

The indigenous Quechua have a tremendous influence on the national identity of Ecuador. Much Ecuadoran visual art portrays elements of indigenous culture, such as farming, llamas, and native dance. The Andes Mountains also form part of the background in many works, as in Hugo Licta's *Indian Dancers and Musicians*. Like many Ecuadoran artists, Licta often depicts the indigenous heritage of his country.

Study *Indian Dancers and Musicians*, *Quechua Village* by Hugo Licta, and answer the following questions.

1. What does Hugo Licta's painting reveal about the culture of the Quechua? What do you think Licta's attitude toward this culture is? Use details from the painting to support your answer.

______

______

______

______

______

2. The depiction of the daily activities of a society can provide a unique insight into its culture. If you were to paint daily routines that were representative of your culture, which activities would you choose? Why would you choose these?

______

______

______

______

Indian Dancers and Musicians (*Quechua Village, Andes*), Hugo Licta. Photograph by Mireille Vautier/The Art Archive.

Nombre ____________________ Clase ____________ Fecha ____________

Fine Art Activities

Las floristas, Camilo Egas

Camilo Egas began his artistic training in his native Ecuador, but later attended art academies in both Spain and France before settling in the United States. Although he lived, painted, and taught in New York, Egas was deeply involved in issues affecting the indigenous population of his homeland. Many of his paintings, including *Las floristas*, depict scenes of indigenous life in Ecuador.

Examine the painting *Las floristas* by Camilo Egas, and answer the following questions with complete sentences.

1. Who or what do you think the focus of the painting is? Why do you think so?

____

____

____

____

____

____

2. Who are the four young women in the painting? What are they doing? Where do you think they are going? Explain your answers with details from the painting.

____

____

____

____

____

____

Las floristas (1916), Camilo Egas. Oil on canvas, 97 cm x 155 cm. Courtesy of Museo Nacional del Banco Central dell Ecuador, Quito.

Nombre _______________ Clase _______________ Fecha _______________

Fine Art Activities

The Rodriguez's, Patssi Valdez

Many artists find inspiration in their immediate surroundings. Patssi Valdez is a Mexican-American artist well-known for her colorful and imaginative paintings, dozens of which depict scenes of kitchens, bedrooms, and other indoor landscapes. The painting *The Rodriguez's* is a vibrant portrayal of a living room.

Study *The Rodriguez's* and complete the following activities.

1. Discuss your impressions of the painting.

a. What is the first thing that strikes you about Valdez's painting? Is it an image? A color? An emotion? Write your answer and explain how what you chose grabbed your attention.

____

____

b. Study the painting closely and mark an X next to the items that appear in the room.

____ A small crucifix

____ A diary

____ A large crucifix

____ Photographs on the wall

____ A garden

____ A blue pillow

____ A patio bench

____ A green-bordered rug

____ A glass of water

____ A couch that recently has been sat upon

2. What do the distinctive room and the things in it tell you about the kind of person who lives here? Describe what you think the owner of this room is like in three complete sentences. Write what you think his or her personality is like and what his or her interests might be.

____

____

Fine Art Activities Answer Key

CANOAS Y CASAS EN EL SUBURBIO, OSWALDO GUAYASAMÍN, page 86

1. Answers will vary. Students should be able to clarify their responses with examples from the painting.

2a. Answers will vary. The painting lacks the details usually associated with human occupancy, e.g. cars, animals, people, clotheslines, etc.

b. Answers will vary.

INDIAN DANCERS AND MUSICIANS, QUECHUA VILLAGE, HUGO LICTA, page 87

1. Answers will vary. Possible answers: People took care of animals such as llamas in their daily lives in the mountains.

2. Answers will vary.

LAS FLORISTAS, CAMILO EGAS, page 88

1. Answers will vary.

2. Answers will vary. Egas's painting depicts women on their way to a traditional celebration in rural Ecuador.

THE RODRIGUEZ'S, PATSSI VALDEZ, page 89

1a. Answers may vary.

b. Marked items should be: A small crucifix; A patio bench; A large crucifix; Photographs on the wall; A couch that recently has been sat upon

2. Answers will vary. Students may focus on the bright colors, the Christian and Eastern religious symbols, the pictures of family members, etc.

Date: ___________

Dear Family:

We are about to begin *Unidad 5* of the Level 1 *¡Avancemos!* program. It focuses on authentic culture and real-life communication using Spanish in Ecuador. It practices reading, writing, listening, and speaking, and introduces students to culture typical of Ecuador.

Through completing the activities, students will employ critical thinking skills as they compare the Spanish language and the culture of Ecuador with their own community. They will also connect to other academic subjects, using their knowledge of Spanish to access new information. In this unit, students are learning to describe houses and household items, indicate the order of things, describe people and locations, plan a party, talk about chores and responsibilities, tell someone what to do, and say what they just did. They are also learning about grammar—the verbs **ser** and **estar**, ordinal numbers, more irregular verbs, affirmative **tú** commands, and **acabar de** + infinitive.

Please feel free to call me with any questions or concerns you might have as your student practices reading, writing, listening, and speaking in Spanish.

Sincerely,

Nombre _______________ Clase _______________ Fecha _______________

Family Involvement Activity

Challenge your brain!

Circles one, three, four, and five each contain a five-letter word and a six-letter word in English. Circle two contains two five-letter words. Circles six and seven contain an eight-letter word and a four-letter word in English. The letters of the two words have been mixed but the left to right order of the letters has not been changed. Find the words.

2. holaumspse

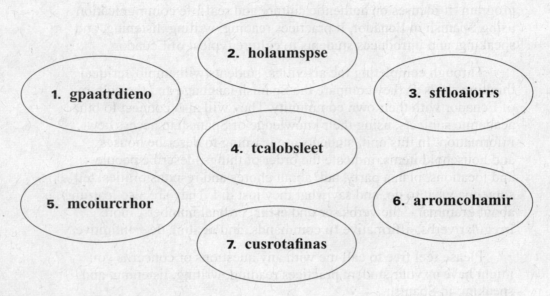

1. gpaatrdieno

3. sftloaiorrs

4. tcalobsleet

5. mcoiurcrhor

6. arromcohamir

7. cusrotafinas

STEP 1

Make a copy of the Mixagrams for each of the participants. Distribute the papers upside down so nobody can read them until you say so.

STEP 2

When you give the signal, all participants turn their papers over and start finding the hidden words. Write as many words as you can in 10 minutes.

STEP 3

The clues are in Spanish in the table below. Fill in the next table with the answers in English so you can all check the answers. Give 1 point for each word found.

Clues to the answers:
1. jardín + patio
2. casa + lámparas
3. escaleras + piso
4. mesa + armario
5. espejo + sofá
6. sillón + cuarto
7. cortinas + sofá

Answers:
1.
2.
3.
4.
5.
6.
7.

Nombre ______________ Clase ______________ Fecha ______________

Absent Student Copymasters

Level 1 pp. 248–250
Level 1B pp. 42–45

Presentación / Práctica de vocabulario

Materials Checklist

- ☐ Student text
- ☐ DVD 2
- ☐ Video activities copymasters
- ☐ TXT CD 5 tracks 1–2
- ☐ L1B TXT CD 1 track 6
- ☐ *Cuaderno* pages 197–199 (L1B pp. 1–3)
- ☐ *Cuaderno para hispanohablantes* pages 197–200 (L1B pp. 1–4)
- ☐ Did You Get It? Copymasters 1, 2, 10

Steps to Follow

- ☐ Study the vocabulary of **Presentación de vocabulario** (pp. 248–249, L1B pp. 42–44) by reading the words above the photos and the accompanying text. Watch the DVD and complete the video activities copymasters.
- ☐ Practice the words of the **Más vocabulario** box on page 249 (L1B p. 44). Read the words aloud. Write the words in your notebook.
- ☐ Listen to the CD as you do the **¡A responder!** activity on page 249 (L1B p. 44).
- ☐ Do **Práctica de vocabulario** (p. 250, L1B p. 45). Complete **Actividades 1** and **2**.
- ☐ Complete *Cuaderno* pages 197, 198, and 199 (L1B pp. 1–3).
OR
Complete *Cuaderno para hispanohablantes* pages 197, 198, 199, and 200 (L1B pp. 1–4).
- ☐ Check your comprehension by completing the **Para y piensa box** on page 250 (L1B p. 45).
- ☐ Complete Did You Get It? Copymasters 1, 2, and 10.

If You Don't Understand . . .

- ☐ Watch the DVD or listen to the CD in a quiet place. If you get lost, stop the DVD or CD and go back.
- ☐ Reread the directions for the activity you find difficult. Write the directions in your own words.
- ☐ Read the model before starting so you know what to do. Follow the model.
- ☐ If the activity has parts for two people, practice both parts.
- ☐ Think about what you are trying to say when you write a sentence. After you write your sentence, check to make sure that it says what you wanted to say.

Absent Student Copymasters

Level 1 pp. 251–252
Level 1B pp. 46–47

Vocabulario en contexto

Materials Checklist

- ☐ Student text
- ☐ DVD 2
- ☐ Video activities copymasters
- ☐ TXT CD 5 track 3
- ☐ Did You Get It? Copymasters 1, 3

Steps to Follow

- ☐ Examine the photos and read the text on page 251 (L1B p. 46).
- ☐ Read **Cuando lees** and **Cuando escuchas** under *Strategies* on page 251 (L1B p. 46). Copy the questions.
- ☐ Answer the questions in **Cuando lees** before watching the DVD.
- ☐ Watch the DVD for **Unidad 5, Telehistoria escena 1** without your book. Then watch the DVD again and complete the video activities copymasters.
- ☐ Look at the dialogue in the book. Follow along in the book as you listen to TXT CD 5 track 3. Use the pictures and context to help you understand the dialogue.
- ☐ Study the words in the **También se dice** box.
- ☐ Complete **Actividades 3**, **4**, and **5** (L1 p. 252, L1B p. 47).
- ☐ Check your comprehension by completing the **Para y piensa box** on page 252 (L1B p. 47).
- ☐ Complete Did You Get It? Copymasters 1 and 3.

If You Don't Understand . . .

- ☐ Watch the DVD in a quiet place. If you get lost, stop the DVD and go back.
- ☐ Listen to the CD in a quiet place. If you get lost, stop the CD and go back.
- ☐ Read the model before starting so you know what to do. Follow the model.
- ☐ If the activity has parts for two people, practice both parts.
- ☐ Think about what you are trying to say when you write a sentence. After you write your sentence, check to make sure that it says what you wanted to say.

Nombre ______________________ Clase ______________ Fecha ______________

Absent Student Copymasters

Level 1 pp. 253–255
Level 1B pp. 48–51

Presentación / Práctica de gramática

Materials Checklist

- ☐ Student text
- ☐ *Cuaderno* pages 200–202 (L1B pp. 4–6)
- ☐ *Cuaderno para hispanohablantes* pages 201–203 (L1B pp. 5–7)
- ☐ TXT CD 5 track 4
- ☐ L1B TXT CD 1 track 7
- ☐ Did You Get It? Copymasters 4, 5, 11, 12
- ☐ ClassZone.com

Steps to Follow

- ☐ Study **ser** and **estar** on page 253 (L1B p. 48).
- ☐ Do **Actividades 6**, **7**, **9**, and **10** on pages 254–255 (L1B pp. 49–50).
- ☐ Complete Actividad 8 using TXT CD 5 track 4 (L1B TXT CD 1 track 7)
- ☐ Complete **Actividades 11** and **12** (L1B p. 51).
- ☐ Complete *Cuaderno* pages 200, 201, and 202 (L1B pp. 4–6).
  OR
  Complete *Cuaderno para hispanohablantes* pages 201, 202, and 203 (L1B pp. 5–7).
- ☐ Check your comprehension by completing the **Para y piensa box** on page 255 (L1B p. 51).
- ☐ Complete Did You Get It? Copymasters 4, 5, 11, and 12.

If You Don't Understand . . .

- ☐ For activities that require listening, listen to the CD in a quiet place. If you get lost, stop the CD and go back.
- ☐ Review the activity directions and study the model. Try to follow the model in your own answers.
- ☐ Read aloud everything that you write. Be sure that you understand what you are reading.
- ☐ Practice both parts of any partner activities.
- ☐ After you write a sentence, check to make sure that it says what you wanted to say.
- ☐ Use the Animated Grammar to help you understand.
- ☐ Use the Leveled Grammar Practice on the @Home Tutor.

Absent Student Copymasters

Level 1 pp. 256–257
Level 1B pp. 52–53

Gramática en contexto

Materials Checklist

- ☐ Student text
- ☐ DVD 2
- ☐ Video activities copymasters
- ☐ TXT CD 5 track 5
- ☐ Did You Get It? Copymasters 4, 6

Steps to Follow

- ☐ Look at the photos on page 256 (L1B p. 52).
- ☐ Read **Cuando lees** and **Cuando escuchas** under *Strategies* on page 256 (L1B p. 52). Copy the questions.
- ☐ Read the script and try to understand the dialogue based on the pictures. Answer the question in **Cuando lees**.
- ☐ Watch the DVD for **Unidad 5, Telehistoria escena 2** without your book. Then watch the DVD again and complete the video activities copymasters.
- ☐ Look at the dialogue in the book. Follow along in the book as you listen to TXT CD 5 track 5. Use the pictures and context to help you understand the dialogue.
- ☐ Study the words in the **También se dice** box.
- ☐ Complete **Actividades 11**, **12**, and **13** (L1 p. 257).
- ☐ Complete **Actividades 13**, **14**, and **15** (L1B p. 53).
- ☐ Check your comprehension by completing the **Para y piensa box** on page 257 (L1B p. 53).
- ☐ Complete Did You Get It? Copymasters 4 and 6.

If You Don't Understand . . .

- ☐ Go to a quiet place and watch the DVD. If you get lost, stop the DVD and go back.
- ☐ Listen to the CD in a quiet place. If you get lost, stop the CD and go back.
- ☐ Reread the activity directions. Write the directions in your own words.
- ☐ Read the model a few times so you are certain that you understand what to do. Follow the model.
- ☐ If the activity has parts for two people, do both parts of the activity.

Nombre ______________________ Clase ______________ Fecha ______________

Absent Student Copymasters

Level 1 pp. 258–260
Level 1B pp. 54–57

Presentación / Práctica de gramática

Materials Checklist

- ☐ Student text
- ☐ *Cuaderno* pages 203–205 (L1B pp. 7–9)
- ☐ *Cuaderno para hispanohablantes* pages 204–207 (L1B pp. 8–11)
- ☐ TXT CD 5 track 6
- ☐ Did You Get It? Copymasters 7, 8, 12
- ☐ ClassZone.com

Steps to Follow

- ☐ Study the ordinal numbers on page 258 (L1B p. 54).
- ☐ Do **Actividades 14** and **15** (L1 p. 259).
- ☐ Do **Actividades 16** and **17** (L1B p. 55).
- ☐ Listen to the TXT CD 5 track 6 as you follow along in the **Pronunciación** activity on p. 259 (L1B p. 56).
- ☐ Complete **Actividad 16** (L1 p. 260).
- ☐ Complete **Actividadades 18**, **19**, and **20** (L1B pp. 55–57).
- ☐ Complete *Cuaderno* pages 203, 204, and 205 (L1B pp. 7–9).
  OR
  Complete *Cuaderno para hispanohablantes* pages 204, 205, 206, and 207. (L1B pp. 8–11).
- ☐ Check your comprehension by completing the **Para y piensa box** on page 260 (L1B p. 57).
- ☐ Complete Did You Get It? Copymasters 7, 8, and 12.

If You Don't Understand . . .

- ☐ Review the section before completing the activities.
- ☐ For activities that require listening, listen to the CD in a quiet place. If you get lost, stop the CD and go back.
- ☐ Write the model on your paper. Try to follow the model in your own answers.
- ☐ Practice both parts of any partner activities.
- ☐ Use the Animated Grammar to help you understand.
- ☐ Use the Leveled Grammar Practice on the @Home Tutor.

Nombre _______________ Clase _______________ Fecha _______________

Absent Student Copymasters

Level 1 pp. 261–263
Level 1B pp. 58–60

Todo junto

Materials Checklist

- ☐ Student text
- ☐ Video activities copymasters
- ☐ DVD 2
- ☐ *Cuaderno* pages 206–207 (L1B pp. 10–11)
- ☐ *Cuaderno para hispanohablantes* pages 208–209 (L1B pp. 12–13)
- ☐ TXT CD 5 tracks 7–9
- ☐ L1B TXT CD 1 tracks 8–9
- ☐ WB CD 3 tracks 1–4
- ☐ HL CD 2 tracks 1–4
- ☐ Did You Get It? Copymasters 7, 9

Steps to Follow

- ☐ Analyze the photos on page 261 (L1B p. 58).
- ☐ Read **Cuando lees** and **Cuando escuchas** under *Strategies* on page 261 (L1B p. 58). Copy the questions.
- ☐ Review the content of **Unidad 5**, **Telehistoria escena 1** and **escena 2**.
- ☐ Read the script and try to understand the dialogue based on the pictures. Answer the question in **Cuando lees**.
- ☐ Listen to the audio for Unidad 5, Telehistoria escena 3 (TXT CD 5 track 7)
- ☐ Watch the DVD for **Unidad 5**, **Telehistoria escena 3** without your book. Then watch the DVD again and complete the video activities copymaster.
- ☐ Complete **Actividades 17**, **18**, **19**, and **21** on pages 262 and 263.
- ☐ Complete **Actividades 21**, **22**, **23**, and **25** (L1B pp. 59–60).
- ☐ Complete **Actividad 20** on page 263 by listening to TXT CD 5 tracks 8, 9 (L1B **Actividad 24**, p. 60, L1B TXT CD 1 tracks 8, 9).
- ☐ Complete *Cuaderno* pages 206 and 207 (L1B pp. 10–11).
  OR
  Complete *Cuaderno para hispanohablantes* pages 208 and 209 (L1B pp. 12–13).
- ☐ Check your comprehension by completing the **Para y piensa box** on page 263 (L1B p. 60).
- ☐ Complete Did You Get It? Copymasters 7 and 9.

Nombre ______________________ Clase ______________ Fecha ______________

Absent Student Copymasters

Level 1 pp. 264–266
Level 1B pp. 62–64

Lectura y Conexiones

Materials Checklist

- ☐ Student text
- ☐ TXT CD 5 track 10

Steps to Follow

- ☐ Read **Strategy: Leer** (L1 p. 264, L1B p. 62).
- ☐ Read **Vivir en Ecuador** on pages 264 and 265 (L1B pp. 62–63).
- ☐ Look at the photos and reread the advertisements.
- ☐ Follow along with the text on TXT CD 5 track 10.
- ☐ Check your comprehension by completing the **¿Comprendiste?** and **¿Y tú?** sections of the **Para y piensa box** on page 265 (L1B p. 63).
- ☐ Read **Los ruinas de Ingapira** on page 266 (L1B p. 64).
- ☐ Read **Proyecto 1, Las ciencias sociales**. Try to complete the activity.
- ☐ Read **La historia** in **Proyecto 2**. Create a map as directed.
- ☐ Read **El lenguaje** in **Proyecto 3**. Try to think of four or five words.

If You Don't Understand . . .

- ☐ Listen to the CD in a quiet place. If you get lost, stop the CD and go back.
- ☐ Reread the directions for the activity you find difficult. Write out the directions in your own words.
- ☐ Read everything aloud. Be sure that you understand what you are reading.
- ☐ Write down any questions you have for your teacher.
- ☐ Think about what you are trying to say when you write a sentence. After you write your sentence, check to make sure that it says what you wanted to say.

Nombre ______________________ Clase ______________ Fecha ______________

Absent Student Copymasters

Level 1 pp. 268–269
Level 1B pp. 66–67

Repaso de la lección

Materials Checklist

- ☐ Student text
- ☐ *Cuaderno* pages 208–219 (L1B pp. 12–23)
- ☐ *Cuaderno para hispanohablantes* pages 210–219 (L1B pp. 14–23)
- ☐ TXT CD 5 track 11
- ☐ L1B TXT CD 1 track 10
- ☐ WB CD 3 tracks 5–10

Steps to Follow

- ☐ Read the bullet points under **¡Llegada!** on page 268. Listen to TXT CD 5 track 11 to complete **Actividad 1** (L1B TXT CD 1 track 10; L1B p. 66).
- ☐ Complete **Actividades 1**, **2**, **3**, **4**, and **5** (L1 pp. 268–269, L1B pp. 66–67).
- ☐ Complete *Cuaderno* pages 208, 209, and 210 (L1B pp. 12–14).
- ☐ Complete *Cuaderno* pages 211, 212, and 213 (L1B pp. 15–17).
  OR
  Complete *Cuaderno para hispanohablantes* pages 210, 211, 212, and 213 (L1B pp. 14–17).
- ☐ Complete *Cuaderno* pages 214, 215, and 216 (L1B pp. 18–20).
  OR
  Complete *Cuaderno para hispanohablantes* pages 214, 215, and 216 (L1B pp. 18–20).
- ☐ Complete *Cuaderno* pages 217, 218, and 219 (L1B pp. 21–23).
  OR
  Complete *Cuaderno para hispanohablantes* pages 217, 218, and 219 (L1B pp. 21–23).

If You Don't Understand . . .

- ☐ Listen to the CD in a quiet place. If you get lost, stop the CD and go back.
- ☐ Reread the directions for the activity you find difficult. Write the directions in your own words.
- ☐ Write the model on your paper. Try to copy the model in your own answers.
- ☐ Say what you want to write before you write it.
- ☐ If you have any questions, write them down for your teacher to answer later.
- ☐ Read your answers out loud to make sure they say what you wanted to say.

Absent Student Copymasters

Level 1 pp. 272–274
Level 1B pp. 70–73

Presentación / Práctica de vocabulario

Materials Checklist

- ☐ Student text
- ☐ DVD 2
- ☐ Video activities copymasters
- ☐ TXT CD 5 tracks 12–13
- ☐ L1B TXT CD 1 track 11
- ☐ *Cuaderno* pages 220–222 (L1B pp. 24–26)
- ☐ *Cuaderno para hispanohablantes* pages 220–223 (L1B pp. 24–27)
- ☐ Did You Get It? Copymasters 13–14

Steps to Follow

- ☐ Study the vocabulary of **Presentación de vocabulario** (pp. 272–273, L1B pp. 70–72) by reading the words above the photos and the accompanying text. Watch the DVD and complete the video activities copymasters.
- ☐ Practice the words of the **Más vocabulario** box on page 272 (L1B p. 72). Read the words aloud. Write the words in your notebook.
- ☐ Do **Práctica de vocabulario** (p. 274, L1B p. 73). Complete **Actividades 1** and **2.**
- ☐ Complete *Cuaderno* pages 220, 221, and 222 (L1B pp. 24–26).
  OR
  Complete *Cuaderno para hispanohablantes* pages 220, 221, 222, and 223 (L1B pp. 24–27).
- ☐ Check your comprehension by completing the **Para y piensa box** on page 274 (L1B p. 73).
- ☐ Complete Did You Get It? Copymasters 13 and 14.

If You Don't Understand . . .

- ☐ Watch the DVD in a quiet place. If you get lost, stop the DVD and go back.
- ☐ Listen to the CD in a quiet place. If you get lost, stop the CD and go back.
- ☐ Reread the directions for the activity you find difficult. Write the directions in your own words.
- ☐ Read the model before starting so you know what to do. Follow the model.
- ☐ If you need a partner to complete the activity, practice both parts.

Nombre ______________ Clase ______________ Fecha ______________

Absent Student Copymasters

Level 1 pp. 275–276
Level 1B pp. 74–75

Vocabulario en contexto

Materials Checklist

- ☐ Student text
- ☐ DVD 2
- ☐ Video activities copymasters
- ☐ TXT CD 5 track 14
- ☐ Did You Get It? Copymasters 13, 15, 22

Steps to Follow

- ☐ Analyze the photo on page 275 (L1B p. 74).
- ☐ Read **Cuando lees** and **Cuando escuchas** under *Strategies* on page 275 (L1B p. 74). Copy the questions.
- ☐ Answer the questions in **Cuando lees** before watching the DVD.
- ☐ Watch the DVD for **Unidad 5, Telehistoria escena 1** without your book. Then watch the DVD again and complete the video activities copymasters.
- ☐ Look at the dialogue in the book. Follow along in the book as you listen to TXT CD 5 track 14. Use the pictures and context to help you understand the dialogue.
- ☐ Complete **Actividades 3** and **4** (L1 p. 276, L1B p. 75).
- ☐ Check your comprehension by completing the **Para y piensa box** on page 276 (L1B p. 75).
- ☐ Complete Did You Get It? Copymasters 13, 15, and 22.

If You Don't Understand . . .

- ☐ Watch the DVD in a quiet place. If you get lost, stop the DVD and go back.
- ☐ Listen to the CD in a quiet place. If you get lost, stop the CD and go back.
- ☐ Reread the directions for the activity you find difficult. Write the directions in your own words.
- ☐ Read the model before starting so you know what to do. Follow the model.
- ☐ If the activity has parts for two people, practice both parts.
- ☐ Think about what you are trying to say when you write a sentence. After you write your sentence, check to make sure that it says what you wanted to say.

Nombre ______________________ Clase ______________________ Fecha ______________________

Absent Student Copymasters

Level 1 pp. 277–279
Level 1B pp. 76–79

Presentación / Práctica de gramática

Materials Checklist

- ☐ Student text
- ☐ *Cuaderno* pages 223–225 (L1B pp. 27–29)
- ☐ *Cuaderno para hispanohablantes* pages 224–226 (L1B pp. 28–30)
- ☐ Did You Get It? Copymasters 16, 17, 22
- ☐ ClassZone.com

Steps to Follow

- ☐ Study the irregular verbs **dar**, **decir**, **poner**, **salir**, **traer**, and **venir** on page 277 (L1B p. 76).
- ☐ Do **Actividades 5**, **6**, **7**, and **8** (L1 pp. 278–279, L1B pp. 77–78).
- ☐ Complete **Actividad 9** (L1B p. 79).
- ☐ Complete *Cuaderno* pages 223, 224, and 225 (L1B pp. 27–29).
  OR
  Complete *Cuaderno para hispanohablantes* pages 224, 225, and 226 (L1B pp. 28–30).
- ☐ Check your comprehension by completing the **Para y piensa box** on page 279. (L1B p. 79).
- ☐ Complete Did You Get It? Copymasters 16, 17, and 22.

If You Don't Understand . . .

- ☐ Reread the activity directions. Write the directions in your own words.
- ☐ Read the model a few times so you are certain that you understand what to do. Follow the model.
- ☐ If the activity has parts for two people, practice both parts.
- ☐ Think about what you are trying to say when you write a sentence. After you write your sentence, check to make sure that it says what you wanted to say.
- ☐ Use the Animated Grammar to help you understand.
- ☐ Use the Leveled Grammar Practice on the @Home Tutor.

Nombre ______________________ Clase ______________ Fecha ______________

Absent Student Copymasters

Level 1 pp. 280–281
Level 1B pp. 80–81

Gramática en contexto

Materials Checklist

- ☐ Student text
- ☐ Video activities copymaster
- ☐ DVD 2
- ☐ TXT CD 5 track 15
- ☐ Did You Get It? Copymasters 16, 18, 23

Steps to Follow

- ☐ Look at the photos on page 280 (L1B p. 80).
- ☐ Read **Cuando lees** and **Cuando escuchas** under *Strategies* on page 280 (L1B p. 80). Copy the questions.
- ☐ Read the script and try to understand the dialogue based on the picture. Answer the questions in **Cuando lees**.
- ☐ Watch the DVD for **Unidad 5, Telehistoria escena 2** without your book. Then watch the DVD again and complete the video activities copymasters.
- ☐ Look at the dialogue in the book. Follow along in the book as you listen to TXT CD 5 track 15. Use the pictures and context to help you understand the dialogue.
- ☐ Study the words in the **También se dice** box.
- ☐ Complete **Actividades 9, 10,** and **11** (L1 p. 281).
- ☐ Complete **Actividades 10, 11,** and **12** (L1B p. 81).
- ☐ Check your comprehension by completing the **Para y piensa box** on page 281 (L1B p. 81).
- ☐ Complete Did You Get It? Copymasters 16, 18, and 23.

If You Don't Understand . . .

- ☐ Go to a quiet place and watch the DVD. If you get lost, stop the DVD and go back.
- ☐ Listen to the CD in a quiet place. If you get lost, stop the CD and go back.
- ☐ Reread the activity directions. Write the directions in your own words.
- ☐ Read the model a few times so you are certain that you understand what to do. Follow the model.
- ☐ If the activity has parts for two people, do both parts of the activity.

Absent Student Copymasters

Level 1 pp. 282–284
Level 1B pp. 82–85

Presentación / Práctica de gramática

Materials Checklist

- ☐ Student text
- ☐ *Cuaderno* pages 226–228 (L1B pp. 30–32)
- ☐ *Cuaderno para hispanohablantes* pages 227–230 (L1B pp. 31–34)
- ☐ TXT CD 5 tracks 16–17
- ☐ L1B TXT CD 1 track 12
- ☐ Did You Get It? Copymasters 19, 20, 24
- ☐ ClassZone.com

Steps to Follow

- ☐ Study the affirmative **tú** commands on page 282 (L1B p. 82).
- ☐ Complete **Actividades 12**, **13**, and **15** (L1 pp. 283–284).
- ☐ Complete **Actividades 13**, **14**, **16**, **17** and **18** (L1B pp. 83–85).
- ☐ Complete **Actividad 14** on page 284 using TXT CD 5 track 17 (L1B **Actividad 15,** p. 83, L1B TXT CD1 track 12).
- ☐ Listen to TXT CD 5 track 16 as you follow along in the **Pronunciación** activity on p. 283.
- ☐ Complete *Cuaderno* pages 226, 227, and 228 (L1B pp. 30–32).
  OR
  Complete *Cuaderno para hispanohablantes* pages 227, 228, 229, and 230 (L1B pp. 31–34).
- ☐ Check your comprehension by completing the **Para y piensa box** on page 284 (L1B p. 85).
- ☐ Complete Did You Get It? Copymasters 19, 20, and 24.

If You Don't Understand . . .

- ☐ For activities that require listening, listen to the CD in a quiet place. If you get lost, stop the CD and go back.
- ☐ Read the model a few times so you are certain that you understand what to do. Follow the model.
- ☐ If the activity has parts for two people, practice both parts.
- ☐ Use the Animated Grammar to help you understand.
- ☐ Use the Leveled Grammar Practice on the @Home Tutor.

Nombre ____________________ Clase ____________ Fecha ____________

Absent Student Copymasters

Level 1 pp. 285–287
Level 1B pp. 86–88

Todo junto

Materials Checklist

- ☐ Student text
- ☐ DVD 2
- ☐ Video activities copymasters
- ☐ *Cuaderno* pages 229–230 (L1B pp. 33–34)
- ☐ *Cuaderno para hispanohablantes* pages 231–232 (L1B pp. 35–36)
- ☐ TXT CD 5 tracks 18–20
- ☐ L1B TXT CD 1 tracks 13–14
- ☐ WB CD 3 tracks 11–14
- ☐ HL CD 2 tracks 5–8
- ☐ Did You Get It? Copymasters 19, 21

Steps to Follow

- ☐ Read **Cuando lees** and **Cuando escuchas** under *Strategies* (p. 285, L1B p. 86). Copy the questions.
- ☐ Review the content of **Unidad 5**, **Telehistoria escena 1** and **escena 2**.
- ☐ Read the script and try to understand the dialogue based on the pictures. Answer the questions in **Cuando lees**.
- ☐ Watch the DVD for **Unidad 5**, **Telehistoria escena 3** without your book. Then watch the DVD again and complete the video activities copymasters.
- ☐ Look at the dialogue in the book. Follow along as you listen to TXT CD 5 track 18. Use the pictures and context to help you understand the dialogue.
- ☐ Complete **Actividades 16**, **17**, **18**, and **20** (L1 pp. 286–287).
- ☐ Complete **Actividades 19**, **20**, **21**, and **23** (L1B pp. 87–88).
- ☐ Complete **Actividad 9**, page 287, TXT CD 5 tracks 19, 20 (L1B **Actividad 22**, p. 88, L1B TXT CD 1 tracks 13, 14).
- ☐ Complete *Cuaderno* pages 229 and 230 (L1B pp. 33–34).
  OR
  Complete *Cuaderno para hispanohablantes* pages 231 and 232 (L1B pp. 35–36).
- ☐ Check your comprehension by completing the **Para y piensa box** on page 287 (L1B p. 88).
- ☐ Complete Did You Get It? Copymasters 19 and 21.

Nombre ______________________ Clase ______________ Fecha ______________

Absent Student Copymasters

Level 1 pp. 288–289
Level 1B pp. 90–91

Lectura cultural

Materials Checklist

- ☐ Student text
- ☐ TXT CD 5 track 21

Steps to Follow

- ☐ Read **Strategy: Leer** (L1 p. 288, L1B p. 90).
- ☐ Read **¡Avanza!** and **Bailes folklóricos de Ecuador y Panamá** on pages 288 and 289 (L1B pp. 90–91).
- ☐ Look at the photos and reread the text.
- ☐ Follow along with the text on TXT CD 5 track 21.
- ☐ Check your comprehension by completing the **¿Comprendiste?** and **¿Y tú?** sections of the **Para y piensa box** on page 289 (L1B p. 91).

If You Don't Understand . . .

- ☐ Listen to the CD in a quiet place. If you get lost, stop the CD and go back.
- ☐ Reread the directions for the activity you find difficult. Write the directions in your own words.
- ☐ Read everything aloud. Be sure that you understand what you are reading.
- ☐ If you have any questions, write them down so you can ask your teacher later.
- ☐ Think about what you are trying to say when you write a sentence. After you write your sentence, check to make sure that it says what you wanted to say.

Nombre ______________________ Clase ______________ Fecha ______________

Absent Student Copymasters

Level 1 p. 290
Level 1B p. 92

Proyectos culturales

Materials Checklist

- ☐ Student text
- ☐ White and colored construction paper
- ☐ Colored pens and pencils
- ☐ Scissors
- ☐ Glue

Steps to Follow

- ☐ Read **Arte textil de Ecuador y Panamá** (L1 p. 290, L1B p. 92).
- ☐ Look at the photo and follow the instructions for making a tapestry design in **Proyecto 1**.
- ☐ Look at the photo and follow the instructions in **Proyecto 2** to create a mola design.
- ☐ Complete **En tu comunidad**.

If You Don't Understand . . .

- ☐ Do the activity you understand first.
- ☐ Reread the directions for the activity you find difficult. Write out the directions in your own words.
- ☐ If you have any questions, write them down so you can ask your teacher later.

Nombre ______________________ Clase ______________________ Fecha ______________________

Absent Student Copymasters

Level 1 pp. 292–293
Level 1B pp. 94–95

Repaso de la lección

Materials Checklist

- ☐ Student text
- ☐ *Cuaderno* pages 231–242 (L1B pp. 35–46)
- ☐ *Cuaderno para hispanohablantes* pages 231–242 (L1B pp. 37–46)
- ☐ TXT CD 5 track 22
- ☐ L1B TXT CD 1 track 15
- ☐ WB CD 3 tracks 15–20

Steps to Follow

- ☐ Read the bullet points under **¡Llegada!** on page 292 (L1B p. 94).
- ☐ Complete **Actividades 1**, **2**, **3**, **4**, and **5** (L1 pp. 292–293; L1B pp. 94–95). Use TXT CD 5 track 22 to complete **Actividad 1**.
- ☐ Complete *Cuaderno* pages 231, 232, and 233 (L1B pp. 35–37).
- ☐ Complete *Cuaderno* pages 234, 235, and 236 (L1B pp. 38–40).
  OR
  Complete *Cuaderno para hispanohablantes* pages 233, 234, 235, and 236 (L1B pp. 37–40).
- ☐ Complete *Cuaderno* pages 237, 238, and 239 (L1B pp. 41–43).
  OR
  Complete *Cuaderno para hispanohablantes* pages 237, 238, and 239 (L1B pp. 41–43).
- ☐ Complete *Cuaderno* pages 240, 241, and 242 (L1B pp. 44–46).
  OR
  Complete *Cuaderno para hispanohablantes* pages 240, 241, and 242 (L1B pp. 44–46).

If You Don't Understand . . .

- ☐ Do the activities you understand first.
- ☐ Listen to the CD as many times as you need to complete the activity.
- ☐ Reread the directions for the activity you find difficult. Write the directions in your own words.
- ☐ Write the model on your paper. Try to copy the model in your own answers.
- ☐ Read aloud everything that you write. Be sure you understand what you are reading.
- ☐ Think about what you are trying to say when you write a sentence. After you write your sentence, check to make sure that it says what you wanted to say.

Nombre ______________________ Clase ______________ Fecha ______________

Absent Student Copymasters

Level 1 **pp. 294–295**
Level 1B **pp. 96–97**

Comparación cultural

Materials Checklist

- ☐ Student text
- ☐ TXT CD 5 track 23

Steps to Follow

- ☐ Look at the photos on pages 294 and 295 (L1B pp. 96–97).
- ☐ Listen to TXT CD 5 track 23 as you read **¡Así celebramos!** on pages 294 and 295 (L1B pp. 96–97).
- ☐ Follow steps 1 and 2 under **Strategy: Escribir**.
- ☐ Complete **Compara con tu mundo** on page 294 (L1B p. 96).

If You Don't Understand . . .

- ☐ Make sure you are in an area where you can concentrate.
- ☐ Listen to the CD as many times as necessary.
- ☐ Reread the directions for the activity you find difficult. Write the directions in your own words.
- ☐ Read everything aloud. Be sure that you understand what you are reading.
- ☐ Write down any questions you have for your teacher.
- ☐ Think about what you are trying to say when you write a sentence. After you write your sentence, check to make sure that it says what you wanted to say.

Absent Student Copymasters

Level 1 pp. 296–297
Level 1B pp. 98–99

Repaso inclusivo

Materials Checklist

- ☐ Student text
- ☐ TXT CD 5 track 24

Steps to Follow

- ☐ Go over the Options for Review, **Actividades 1**, **2**, **3**, **4**, **5**, **6**, and **7** (L1 pp. 296–297, L1B pp. 98–99).
- ☐ Listen to TXT CD 5 track 24 for **Actividad 1** on page 296 (L1B p. 98). Answer the questions.
- ☐ Give orders to a robot for **Actividad 2** on page 296 (L1B p. 98).
- ☐ Have a yard sale and create a flier for **Actividad 4** on page 296 (L1B p. 98).
- ☐ Complete **Actividad 7** (L1 p. 297, L1B p. 99).

If You Don't Understand . . .

- ☐ Do the activities you understand first.
- ☐ Listen to the CD as many times as you need to complete **Actividad 1**.
- ☐ Reread the directions for the activity you find difficult. Write out the directions in your own words.
- ☐ Say what you want to write before you write it.
- ☐ If you have any questions, write them down so you can ask your teacher later.
- ☐ Practice both parts of any partner activities.
- ☐ After you write a sentence, check to make sure that it says what you wanted to say.